Living Scripture

*is a Path Book
offering practical spirituality
to enrich everyday living.*

*"Your word is a lamp to my feet
and a light to my path."*
Psalm 119:105

for Patti and Niall
and the boys,
Declan, Finn, and Conall,
with love

Living Scripture
The Guidance of God
on the Journey of Life

Herbert O'Driscoll

Path Books
A LIGHT TO MY PATH

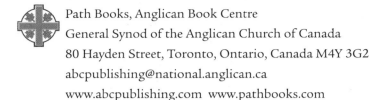

Path Books, Anglican Book Centre
General Synod of the Anglican Church of Canada
80 Hayden Street, Toronto, Ontario, Canada M4Y 3G2
abcpublishing@national.anglican.ca
www.abcpublishing.com www.pathbooks.com

Text set in ITC Legacy Serif Book
Cover and text design by Jane Thornton

Library and Archives of Canada Cataloguing in Publication

O'Driscoll, Herbert, 1928-
Living scripture : the guidance of God on the journey of
life / Herbert O'Driscoll.
Sequel to God with us.
ISBN 1-55126-436-6
1. Bible. O.T.—Biography—Meditations.
2. Stress (Psychology)—Religious aspects—Christianity.
3. Christian life--Anglican authors. I. O'Driscoll, Herbert, 1928- .
God with us. II. Title.

BS571.O375 2005   221.9'22   C2004-906892-
X

Contents

Introduction

The collect for the Second Sunday of Advent in the *Book of Common Prayer* states that God "hast caused all holy scriptures to be written for our learning." While this statement is certainly true, we may sometimes feel like asking the question, "Learning what?"

I have always felt that an answer to this question can be given in fairly simple terms. I say *an* answer because I am under no illusion that there can be any such thing as *the* answer to such a question. Learning whatever God wishes me to learn is at the very least the work of a lifetime, if not of all eternity. However, I still want to find some reasonably simple words to express what God wishes me to learn in a lifetime and beyond.

I think that scripture has been given to us so that we may learn how to live life wisely, fully, and joyfully. When I explore scripture, I encounter men and women who are trying to do precisely this and, just like you and me, quite often failing and sometimes, by the grace of God, going on.

When I read scripture, I notice that the lives of the people in its pages resemble mine. As they live out the full spectrum of human experience, they also express the full spectrum of human emotion. And this is why I find scripture endlessly fascinating. Especially so, because I sometimes have a secret wish to change the ancient collect to something like "God has caused all holy scriptures to be written to make it possible for us to encounter fascinating people, thus learning how to—and how not to—live our own lives."

Recently, I was leafing through the pages of *Genesis,* a wonderful book that emerged from Bill Moyers's television series of the same name. In his introduction, Moyers writes that the more we talk about the people of the Bible, the more they look like people we know—faces in a mirror.

This describes admirably my own experience as I was writing these pages. Throughout them I make an assumption. I assume that scripture is full of lessons, insights, warnings, guidelines, and directions—not to mention invitations, encouragements, and inspirations. I assume that we can receive all these things if only we stop thinking of scripture as being long ago and all about holy people utterly unlike us who have become flattened and one-dimensional in between its pages.

Of course, they wore different clothes and lived in different houses—some in no houses at all—but otherwise they wrestled with the conundrums of life as we have to, laughing and crying and suffering and loving their way through life as we have to, at times wondering as we do what it all means, and doing their best to trust in a God who gives and takes life, and is loving and faithful in between.

The plan of this book is simple. I have grouped together men and women whose lives show us a certain truth about human experience. There are eight of these groups, and each group is introduced by a short reflection. I invite you to meet these people. If meeting them allows us to see that we have the guidance of God on our life's journey, then I will, at least by my own measuring, have succeeded in the work.

Herbert O'Driscoll

Thinking Creatively

Buckminster Fuller kept on asking a question for much of his life. It was about space and how best to enclose it. His response was the geodesic dome, and the most impressive of such domes was seen at Montreal's Expo in 1967. In one leap Fuller had gone beyond all previous designs for enclosing space. He had literally gone "outside the box."

In the fiercely competitive world of today, great importance is given—and great rewards are earned—for the kind of thinking and planning that can point to a new way through the complexities faced in most fields. Very often rich rewards go not necessarily to people who have a great deal of knowledge, but to those who are highly intuitive, who can take mental leaps that land them beyond the problem to a solution. Sometimes this will not itself provide the solution, but it will contain the seeds that make progress possible.

For a Christian the source of all inspiration is the Holy Spirit. It follows that we should expect examples of intuitive leaps in holy scripture.

The apostle Peter suddenly finds himself in a situation for which there is no neat plan, no book of rules to which he can refer. He is also alone; no helpful consultation is possible. So Peter makes a decision. It's a far-reaching one for the new Christian faith. It will get him into trouble because the community is nowhere near a consensus about these things. In fact, the community has not even begun to face such eventualities!

Peter has no choice. He must respond one way or the other. In this predicament he leaps over barriers and exclusions he has taken for granted all his life. We might ask an old if whimsical question. Did he leap, or was he in fact pushed—by God's Holy Spirit?

Isaiah is in the same situation as the rest of his people. For the moment he and they are trapped in exile in Babylon. The difference between Isaiah and everyone else is that they believe they are trapped, and Isaiah begs to differ. The reason could be put in different kinds of language—the language of politics perhaps. But it could also be put in the language of the Spirit.

Isaiah possesses a vision of God that is greater than any particular moment of history and greater than any empire, even the empire that at the moment holds him and his people prisoner. Because of this large vision of God, Isaiah is able to possess a large geopolitical vision. His mind extends beyond even the far-flung borders of Babylon to see a distant leader as nothing less than God's instrument to achieve Israel's freedom.

Ezekiel is with the same people in the same situation of exile and oppression. For him, the way out of a sense of imprisonment comes by way of a dream. He would be neither the first nor the last to be addressed in a dream by the Spirit of God. One of the great poems of the romantic period, *Kubla Khan*, came fully formed to Samuel Taylor Coleridge in a dream. Many of Carl Jung's inspirations about psychotherapy came in the form of dreams. Such dreams took these and others beyond the seeming limitations of some problem or situation or pattern, allowing them to find a path forward.

Here are three people enabled by the Spirit to take leaps of discernment and new vision. They are by no means alone in holy scripture. There are others potentially among them—ourselves!

~ 1 ~

A Leap in Faith

While Peter was still speaking, the Holy Spirit fell upon all who heard the word. The circumcised believers who had come with Peter were astounded that the gift of the Holy Spirit had been poured out even on the Gentiles.... Then Peter said, "Can anyone withhold the water for baptizing these people who have received the Holy Spirit just as we have?" So he ordered them to be baptized in the name of Jesus Christ. Acts 10:44–48

Suggested reading: Acts of the Apostles 10

One of the ironies of Western culture is that we have come to regard everything as being in a state of flux—whether it be the concepts or the processes by which society is formed. But we have difficulty regarding our personal spirituality as an ongoing living process. The last few centuries have made us forget that Christian faith is not merely a set of propositions to be believed but a relationship with God to which we give ourselves in trust. We assume that Christian faith remains the same once we have received it. And we can get rather angry with anybody or anything that challenges what we believe and the way we believe it. The idea that God might be asking us to understand our relationship with the divine in new ways can be deeply disturbing.

It is all the more moving when we see someone liberated from the wish to keep their relationship with God within the understandings they have had since childhood. The Bible gives us portraits of more than one such person, but for now, we encounter a magnificently courageous middle-aged man.

It is only months after the extraordinary few days that had witnessed the crucifixion and subsequent resurrection of Jesus. The small community of his followers is still wrestling with what the consequences may be for them. Peter has gone to the coast and obtained lodgings, first in Lydda and then in Joppa. It looks as if he was seeking to reassure and encourage those few who had already been drawn into an allegiance with the crucified and risen Jesus.

Peter's own life will be changed radically before his visit to the coast is over. He does not know it, but some miles to the north a deeply religious Roman officer has just had a vivid and life-changing dream. In his vision he feels himself directed to send south to Joppa for a man of whom he has no previous knowledge, one called Simon Peter. Cornelius wakes and acts. That very day he dispatches three men to invite Peter to Caesarea.

Meanwhile, as the three are nearing Joppa, Peter lies down to rest in the heat of the afternoon and has his own life-changing vision. In his dream, food of every conceivable kind is offered to him. His Jewish instincts rebel against much of it. Sternly he is ordered to refrain from calling unclean what God has created as clean! Peter awakes troubled and puzzled.

No sooner has he woken than the three men from Caesarea appear at his door, telling him of Cornelius's invitation. Begging for time to form a response to this utterly unexpected event, Peter asks them to give him the night to consider. The next day the four of them head north.

Perhaps we should remind ourselves of the position Peter has placed himself in, merely by accepting this invitation. He is going to the house not only of a Gentile—a despised outsider—but also of one who represents the oppressive Roman occupation of his country. Even to stand in the atrium of Cornelius's house and accept his greeting is trespassing on the conventions of acceptable Jewish behaviour.

What Peter hears from Cornelius's warm welcome must at first have been beyond belief. Here was this Gentile claiming the direct guidance of God, and then requesting Peter's guidance as to what he and his household should do!

With difficulty Peter gathers his whirling thoughts. Probably without making a conscious decision to do so, he finds himself telling his small rapt audience about the events of the last few years in his life, especially the unbelievable weekend of the crucifixion—inflicted by his host's own military power—and his certainty of Jesus' resurrection. As Peter speaks, he also notices their response. He sees nothing less than the power of God's Holy Spirit affecting this family and their household!

Peter himself is so moved by this undeniable manifestation of God's Holy Spirit that he is swept up into the almost inexpressible joy and fervour all around him. Perhaps hardly believing what he hears himself say, he calls for the group to receive baptism. And in that moment, not only does Peter's life and ministry change forever, but the course of the new faith takes a massive turn toward a future of inclusion. In time Peter would have to justify his action before others. By no means would it meet with universal approval, but there would be no going back.

Joppa, Caesarea, and the house of Cornelius are long ago, but the issues played out in that house remain with us. Christians are constantly being challenged by God to respond to the new visions that God offers. Most often these challenges are given to us in terms of stepping across boundaries previously regarded as ultimate. These boundaries take various forms, sometimes racial and cultural. One by one such boundaries are crossed as the Holy Spirit impels.

In recent decades we have met many boundaries, some in the area of new medical possibilities and some in the area of human sexuality. We stand in the kind of moment that Peter experienced in that long-ago home. When we feel resentful that such difficult choices are given to us, we need to remember that many before us have stood at what seemed like ultimate boundaries, and they have had to decide whether or not God was impelling them to step into new realities.

~ 2 ~

A Larger God

Listen to me in silence, O coastlands ... Who has roused a victor from the east, summoned him to his service? He delivers up nations to him, and tramples kings under foot.... Thus says the Lord to his anointed, to Cyrus, whose right hand I have grasped to subdue nations before him and strip kings of their robes.... For the sake of my servant Jacob, and Israel my chosen, I call you by your name, I surname you, though you do not know me. Isaiah 41:1–2; 45:1–4

Suggested reading: Isaiah 41:1–10 and 45:1–8

Great corporations value those who have administrative and organizational gifts. Accountants, planners, managers, all contribute to the success of the enterprise. Yet more and more in these highly competitive days, other gifts are being sought, gifts that are almost the opposite of the above. One phrase that has become popular to describe these gifts is "thinking outside the box," developing the ability to go beyond the logical, the familiar, the tried and true.

In the fifth century BCE, Israel suffered what for any society is a devastating blow. Their capital, Jerusalem, was attacked by a powerful enemy—a superpower of that long-ago time—and was left a smoking ruin. Thousands were slaughtered, and tens of thousands were taken into exile. As the years went by, those who had been exiled began to deal with this new reality of their lives in different ways. Some slowly won for themselves a place in Babylonian society. Others lapsed into despondency or seethed with helpless anger. Most assumed that life in their beloved country was over for the foreseeable future, and that they themselves were fated to die in exile. The empire that had conquered them was showing no signs of weakening; nor was there the slightest indication that its foreign policy would relax and let them return to their distant homeland.

But quite unknown to most of them, there was among them, sharing their exile, a man of the most extraordinary breadth of vision. We know his name as Isaiah. The evidence suggests that he was attuned to every nuance of the surrounding society, listening to the many voices around him and piecing together a picture of the situation in which he and his people seemed to be trapped.

We do not know the moment when Isaiah realized that he and his people might not actually be trapped, that in fact things were very different from what most of his compatriots presumed. But we do have a record of the first time he dropped a hint of hope. He cannot yet name names, but he can point to certain recent events indicating that great changes are possible. "Listen to me in silence," he says, and then asks a cryptic question, "Who has roused a victor from the east?"

Having discerned a presentiment of things to come, Isaiah has to wait for more information to be precise. But the moment comes for such precision. By this time it is quite probable that rumblings of large events have reached the streets and alleyways of the ghetto. The name now on everyone's lips is that of Cyrus, a Persian leader who is attacking at the edge of the Babylonian empire.

At this stage Isaiah goes beyond accepted thinking. He points to Cyrus as the very instrument of God to bring freedom to the people of God in their exile. Those who hear Isaiah are astonished. How can this unbeliever, Cyrus, be of any consequence at all in the designs of God? Isaiah's response shows how limited such thinking is, how limited their view of God is. God is far more than the God of a single small people. As they listen to him, Isaiah rolls back the bounds of their imagination and understanding. "I am the Lord, and there is no other," he says of God. "I form light and create darkness.... I the Lord do all these things."

Isaiah's grasp of the changing geopolitics of his time proves to be true. The Babylonian empire falls. Cyrus takes over and brings into being an utterly different foreign policy, one that is not prepared to tolerate a political vacuum on the western borders, where Egypt can wreak much mischief. Very soon after Cyrus assumes full control, a royal decree emerges, ordering a return of the exiled to Jerusalem with the express intention of rebuilding the city.

Not only did this announcement come as a shattering surprise, it was positively unwelcome news to those who had done quite well for themselves in their new land. They had no wish to return to a frontier existence, probably offering nothing but endless hard work and considerable danger from those who had long since taken over lands vacated by the exiles. However, a sufficient number of hardy souls was found to form the homeward caravan. In due time an expedition was heading west to rebuild their country. With them went the authority of the royal proclamation, supplies for the task ahead, a Persian governor, and a reassuring squadron of imperial troops.

It is instructive to remind ourselves that the information Isaiah gathered and used to motivate his people was probably available to others. What made the difference was Isaiah's prior conviction that, with God, all was possible. More than anything else it was this conviction that brought him to his intuitive leap about the true significance of Cyrus and his campaign.

Is this the secret of our ability to extend the bounds of the possible? Even when we do not use the language of religion and instead use expressions such as "thinking outside the box," are we in fact intuiting at a deep level that we live in a universe of infinite possibility, precisely because it is the creation of the God in whom all things are possible?

~ 3 ~

A Dream of the Future

"And you shall know that I am the Lord, when I open your graves, and bring you up from your graves, O my people. I will put my spirit within you, and you shall live, and I will place you on your own soil; then you shall know that I, the Lord, have spoken and will act," says the Lord. Ezekiel 37:13–14

Suggested reading: Book of Ezekiel, 37:1–14

Jürgen Moltmann has pointed out that there are two Latin words for the future—*futurum* and *adventus*. *Futurum* he calls "the future of social calculation." By this he means a vision of the future that we form from our own observations, our studying of trends, our extrapolation from present patterns. Many businesses and institutions spend large sums of money on such futurizing.

But, Moltmann points out, there is also *adventus*, what he calls "the future of ethical anticipation." By this he means a future that comes toward us from beyond us and is not in any sense in our control. This is the future that we try to envision when we ask the question, What do we hope for in the future we are trying to envision?

The extraordinary minds whom we know as the prophets of ancient Israel were past masters at communicating what Moltmann has called *adventus*. As we listen to one of them, the person we know as the prophet Ezekiel, we realize the extraordinary effect of this power to envision the future.

The situation is one of prolonged national exile. A number of years have passed since the newly risen Babylonian empire had attacked Israel, destroyed Jerusalem, and taken thousands away captive. Many have settled by the river Chebar, a part of the gigantic delta of the Tigris and Euphrates river system.

Working within Babylonian society—where some subsisted as forced labourers and others eventually managed to build small businesses—they desperately kept alive the hope of one day returning home and rebuilding Jerusalem. Eventually some decided to jettison this hope and to settle in the new land. Some simply refused to give up hope.

When things are at a particularly low ebb, Ezekiel, himself an exile, finds some public occasion to address his own people. With them he shares a dream. At first it has all the trappings of a nightmare. He relates how he has dreamed that he is looking over a dry, utterly barren, sand-strewn valley. He continues to look until he discerns white protrusions in the sand. To his horror he realizes that he is gazing at a sea of human bones. The valley is full of death!

In his dream Ezekiel hears God asking a question, "Can these bones live?" Ezekiel cannot dare to answer. Helplessly he stammers out, "O Lord God, you know." But God does not accept Ezekiel's response of helplessness. Ezekiel is encouraged, even ordered, to address the situation, step by careful step. To his astonishment his first disbelieving words have immediate effect. The bones move. They begin to form patterns that eventually become human in outline. As he watches, both horrified and fascinated, a great host of human-like figures, frozen in stillness, forms before his eyes.

Ezekiel realizes that he is seeing the form of life without life itself. Again he hears an inner voice calling him to take initiative, to call the forms into life, to give them breath. We can almost hear the wonder in Ezekiel's voice—and in the eyes and minds of those listening to him—as he tells what happens. "I prophesied as [God] commanded me, and the breath came into them, and they lived, and stood on their feet, a vast multitude!"

Then, in what must have been utter silence among his listeners, Ezekiel begins to address the loneliness, the fears, the hopelessness of this exiled people. With slow deliberation—in language rich, vivid, and powerful—he explains what his dream has told him. "These bones are the whole house of Israel. They say, 'Our bones are dried up.'"

Then in tones that must have rung out over the listening crowd, Ezekiel lifts his voice and calls out as loudly as he can, enunciating every word with passionate deliberation: "Thus says the Lord God: I am going to open your graves ... O my people; and I will bring you back to the land of Israel."

As we know, Ezekiel's dream eventually came true. The day arrived when some of the more enterprising among them left Babylon to cross the endless miles west. In time they passed over the desert, forded the Jordan river, and climbed the escarpment to find themselves looking at the ruins of their beloved Jerusalem. But it is highly unlikely that any of this would have happened had it not been for the power of a vision such as Ezekiel's, not to mention his God-given gift of expressing this vision in a way that could energize his listeners.

In recent decades we have seen again and again something emerging in societies around the world. Once the dream of a better future has come into the mind of a people—a dream of liberation, of justice, of a better life—it has repeatedly proved unstoppable. Guns, tanks, prisons, torture—all fail in their effects. The dream of a possible future seems to send a pulse of energy into the present, so that the dreamed-of future begins to be born.

This truth can be experienced in our own lives. The dream of a better future can enliven our hearts and minds, and galvanize us into action to bring about that future. The vision of better health or a more rewarding career can inspire such determination and resolve that eventually we realize surprising change. God can work mysteriously and powerfully in our dreams. Far from being an indication of passivity, the words "I have a dream" can become a prelude to new life.

The Challenge of Leadership

One of the staples for journalists who write about business and corporate affairs is the subject of leadership. Every conceivable aspect of leadership is explored. Interviews are given by those already far up the corporate ladder. Retired CEOs reminisce about the challenges that leadership must face, as they recall with relish how they triumphed in the fray! Recipes for success are sought and supplied. The subject is never exhausted.

It would be strange if the subject of leadership did not emerge again and again in scripture. Here I describe five examples.

As a leader Moses towers over the Old Testament landscape. He remains larger than life all through the life of Judaism. Beyond Judaism, Moses and the desert journey linked with his name have become the template for all sorts of reflection about institutions and organizations in transition. Even the obvious humanity of the man, revealed on more than one occasion, does not diminish him, but emphasizes the human cost of his great achievements.

In Deborah we see another kind of leadership. She is asked to lead in a markedly different way than she has done before. Instead of refusing heavy responsibility, she realizes that she can apply her gifts, but that other gifts are also needed. She then proceeds to look for human resources—as we would say today. In someone very different from herself she finds help. Together their gifts prove to provide exactly the mixture needed for success.

The episode of David at the well in Bethlehem depicts a young man already showing signs of being a natural leader. At this moment in David's early campaigning we see a quality not always present in the early stages of a career. There is a sensitivity to others that goes far in strengthening the bonds between leader and those led.

In Jeremiah the prophet we again discern the cost of being a leader. We see someone almost dragged to accept leadership, a man agonizing about what he should say and do. We encounter those contradictory feelings that make us all so human—fear and courage, acceptance and resentment, despair and hope—all mingled in Jeremiah.

A letter written by the apostle Peter was circulated to the early Christian churches scattered around the Mediterranean. The situation calling for the letter was grim. It had become costly and dangerous to belong to the new faith. Leadership was desperately needed and sought. The elderly Peter was exactly the right person. His suggested responses to the current stresses were couched in utterly simple and direct, even blunt, language. They go straight to the heart of what makes a strong community. Every word is as relevant today as it ever was.

~ 4 ~

Facing the Wilderness

The whole congregation of the Israelites complained against Moses and Aaron in the wilderness.... Then the Lord said to Moses, "I am going to rain bread from heaven for you, and each day the people shall go out and gather enough for that day."... Then Moses said to Aaron, "Say to the whole congregation of the Israelites, 'Draw near to the Lord, for he has heard your complaining.'" Aaron spoke to the whole congregation ... they looked toward the wilderness, and the glory of the Lord appeared in the cloud.

Exodus 16:2–10

Suggested reading: Exodus 16:1–12

M uch of the stress and conflict in organizations and institutions come from the unceasing process of change. For many reasons inherent in the times, change is universal and unavoidable. Its effects are many and varied—some positive, some negative. Whatever the effects may be, there is always a certain amount of stress in managing change. It is quite extraordinary the degree to which the Exodus story has become, in recent years, a metaphor for this period of immense transition.

The Exodus journey of the Jewish people, taking them from captivity to freedom, is still in its early days, yet already the journey is beginning to have its effects. The first novelty has worn off. The desert and its climate, the need to keep on the move each day, the scarce supplies of food—all are beginning to take their toll. What begins now is what always happens when any group of human beings is responding to pressure. Voices start to focus on the leadership, not always in a complimentary way. Things that have been forgiven to this point are now dredged up as an excuse for criticism.

Israel is no exception. A measure of self-pity creeps in; resentment begins to fester. Soon this comes into the open. Moses and his brother Aaron and their sister Miriam find themselves being blamed for the problems of the people.

At first their leadership is faulted for not solving all the problems. But then a more ominous tone creeps in. Perhaps in a group around Moses and Aaron, or maybe in a large open meeting of tribal leaders, the pent-up resentment and dissatisfaction erupts. A voice shouts its suspicion that they were all brought into this ghastly wilderness to die. The leadership stands accused of being not just ineffective—such criticism is to be expected. The voices are suggesting something much more dangerous to the whole enterprise. They are saying that the leadership is actually their enemy. Trust itself is breaking down.

It is interesting to see how Moses responds. He is aware of one thing that is not yet generally known. He probably learned it during the years he spent in this same wilderness looking after his father-in-law's flocks. Moses knows that it is possible, with any luck, for these people to live off this land—not a luxurious life perhaps, but a life at least. This he proceeds to tell them.

Here we see two things at work that contribute to the quality of Moses' leadership. First, he discerns the simple reason for the groundswell of discontent. It is an immediate physical problem, and it can be dealt with practically. Second, he has experience, and this makes him a first-class leader in the situation. Quite literally, he has been here before.

But Moses also sees that nothing in life is merely practical. There are always other reasons for human reactions. Moses knows that the problem is not just physical hunger. There is another kind of hunger—a hunger of morale and a hunger for hope. He does something again very simple but wonderfully effective. He assembles the people and makes them stand in such a way that they are looking out over the wilderness ahead of them. It is one of the most powerful moments in the entire Hebrew scriptures.

"The whole congregation of the Israelites ... looked toward the wilderness, and the glory of the Lord appeared in the cloud." Then Moses addresses them. We probably do not know all that he said, but one thing shows him thinking very wisely about the nature of leadership. "Your complaining," says Moses, "is not against us but against the Lord." In this passage from the Exodus journey, we are being given insight into the human dynamics of a period of transition. These dynamics affect everyone, whether or not they have accepted the responsibility of leadership.

Everyone today is in some way on a wilderness journey through a period of transition. Every level of our human experience is affected—personal life, relationships, professional life. Trying to run from this experience is self-defeating. It only adds to our feelings of helplessness and threat. Only if we stand and face the wilderness, its issues and challenges, do we have some chance of winning through.

In this passage we are also being reminded about one of the most important requirements for anyone to survive successfully in a position of leadership. Because a leader is often visible and even accessible, people's reactions are aimed in his or her direction. But the one thing a leader must not do is to take personally the emotions that are bound to erupt in great and constant change. Obviously this is easier to say than do, but it is essential for leadership survival.

Anger and resentment are directed at a leader because—justified or not—he or she is regarded as the source of change. While many in their rational moments may realize that the leader is actually not the source, and that he or she must also be under tremendous stress, the intensity of their emotions precludes much rational thinking. When a leader acknowledges that the situation is larger than oneself and, like Moses, seeks God's guidance, a way can open in the wilderness.

～5～

Courage Under Fire

The Israelites again did what was evil in the sight of the Lord, after Ehud died. So the Lord sold them into the hand of King Jabin of Canaan, who reigned in Hazor; the commander of his army was Sisera.... Then the Israelites cried out to the Lord for help.... At that time Deborah, a prophetess, wife of Lappidoth, was judging Israel. Judges 4:1–4

Suggested reading: Book of Judges 4

Successful management in any field depends on making certain important choices. Perhaps the most important of such choices are about who will work with us as colleagues. There is a trap we can very easily fall into. Human nature makes us wish to have around us people like ourselves. This way we can relax and trust. We can be sure that things will be done the way we wish.

But this neat solution is fraught with danger. A group of people all sharing much the same pattern of strengths can be, of course, reassuringly comfortable. But it can also be surprisingly, even fatally, vulnerable. What leads to the prospering of any enterprise is not building successive layers of the same gifts, but building an organization of many different gifts. We may not be as comfortable with people whose very different gifts challenge and correct us, but we will be better served, and what we are trying to accomplish will have a much better chance of success.

We see this wisdom at work in the decisions and actions of an extraordinary woman who lived in northern Galilee in the twelfth century BCE. Her name was Deborah. She occupied a place in her society that is a little difficult to define in terms of our own world. Scripture tells us that Deborah was a judge. We tend to think of wigs, gowns, gavels, and the decorum of a modern courtroom. We would be mistaken, but not wholly wrong. Deborah, as a judge in that long-ago society, would indeed have sat in judgement on disputes. However, her authority would have rested not on any judicial system, but on the respect in which her society held her. She was recognized as a woman of immense insight, wisdom, and integrity. This explains her influence and role among her people.

Deborah's life changes one day when her community asks

her to take on a role for which she has no obvious gifts. They implore her to lead an army to rescue them from a neighbouring bully who has tormented and terrorized them for as long as some can remember. For twenty years Jabin and his powerful forces have kept a stranglehold on the richest tract of land in Israel—the Jezreel Valley—a lush and productive area that runs from west to east between the highlands of Galilee and the Samaria hills.

This request to Deborah is a measure of the trust and respect felt for her by her people. She does not immediately commit herself, but she takes a preliminary and all-important decision. Although she has the very antithesis of a military mind, she knows exactly where to find such a first-class mind. She turns to Barak, a man with a proven military track record and knowledge of Jabin's terrain. When the two meet, Barak's response is in itself a magnificent tribute to the respect in which Deborah is held.

He accepts the challenge but only on one condition. "If you will go with me," says this tough soldier, "I will go; but if you will not go with me, I will not go." We can hear the plain blunt manner in every word. We can also hear the inner security that allowed this man to say this to a woman in this society where many men would have hesitated to express any such dependency.

That Deborah is sensitive to his regard for her is shown by an interesting warning she gives to Barak. She tells him that Jabin's general, Sisera, will die not directly by his campaign, but by the hand of a woman. We can only surmise whether Deborah was already planning such an eventuality. Again it is interesting that Barak accepts this arrangement without question—yet another indication of his respect for this woman who has sought his help in this heavy responsibility.

So Deborah and Barak go to war, a battle they have no guarantee of winning, other than Deborah's deep conviction that the Lord in whom she trusts will not betray them. Building on her own reputation, she forms a confederation of local tribes, and eventually they return victorious. During the battle it is Barak who plans tactics and strategy while Deborah builds morale. Their partnership will be celebrated down the years in the song attributed to both of them. "Awake, awake, Deborah! Awake, awake, utter a song! Arise, Barak, lead away your captives, O son of Abinoam."

From our vantage point we see an enterprise become successful because it is undertaken with a rich mixture of human gifts. Wise planning goes hand in hand with courageous action. But the really wise insight we see in Deborah's strategy is her immediate recognition that she needs someone utterly unlike herself with an utterly different set of strengths.

In our own projects and plans, success begins when we realize that we cannot always succeed in a particular enterprise alone. We may not do our best by gathering around us people too much like ourselves. But it takes inner security to invite people with gifts differing from our own. If we entertain fears of being upstaged, then the enterprise can be fatally flawed. Choosing one's help well is all-important. In the wedding of differences lies success.

For a Christian there is another factor. If our enterprise is laid before God in prayer, and if our prayer is not merely asking for success but rather offering our work to God so that his will may be done through it, and if our prayer is also asking for guidance in the work—then we may gain a sense of grace about what we are doing that will strengthen and enrich the whole endeavour.

~ 6 ~

Recognizing Loyalty

Three ... chiefs went down to the rock to David at the cave of Adullam, while the army of Philistines was encamped in the valley of Rephaim. David was then in the stronghold; and the garrison of the Philistines was then at Bethlehem. David said longingly, "O that someone would give me water to drink from the well of Bethlehem that is by the gate!"

Then the Three broke through the camp of the Philistines, and drew water from the well of Bethlehem that was by the gate, and they brought it to David. But David would not drink of it; he poured it out to the Lord, and said ... "Can I drink the blood of these men? For at the risk of their lives they brought it." Therefore he would not drink it.

1 Chronicles 11:15–19

Suggested reading: 1 Chronicles 11:10–19

The devil, some say, is in the details. But sometimes so is God, especially when it comes to human character and personality. There can be moments in our relationships with others when, in a flash, we learn volumes about a person normally hidden behind the mask that, to some extent, we all wear. When such a moment happens in the lives of the prominent and powerful, it can be all the more revealing.

We are in the hill country south of where Jerusalem lies today. It is just before the meteoric rise of David to political and military power. He has by no means yet consolidated that power. He is little more than a fugitive on the run, staying alive by keeping one jump ahead of Saul's pursuing troops. High up on the rocky spine of the country, some miles behind him to the north, is a dusty hill fortress held by a tribe called the Jebusites. A day will come when David will lay siege to this fortress and eventually conquer it, making it his royal palace and headquarters. The future will look back on it as David's royal city, a name much grander than the early actuality.

At present David is engaged in another skirmish with the people who seem to have been his most stubborn rivals for power. The Philistines, pushing in from the coast, now hold the area. With the strategic skill that has made them a formidable enemy to Israel, they have holed up in the village of Bethlehem. David and his ragtag band of guerrillas are in the surrounding countryside.

One of the luxuries of power—as David would come to learn and possess in later years—is the ability to choose when you fight your wars. You march when the harsh climate of the area is most conducive to vigorous activity—probably in spring and fall. But at this stage in his life David is clawing for power. He does not have the luxury of choosing times or places for battle. He must fight when threatened or to stake out territory. This is one of those times.

One of David's great gifts was his ability to attract others to his causes. There was something about him that inspired loyalty, and we are about to witness a moment that goes a long way toward explaining his attraction.

In a dry harsh climate, basically a semi-desert climate, drinking water can be hard and sometimes almost bitter. The quality of well water varies from place to place. For some reason, the well in Bethlehem had a reputation for the quality of its water. Obviously, David remembered drinking from it at some point in the past. The fact that he knows its exact location—"by the gate"—would suggest this.

At some unguarded moment David expresses a longing for a drink from the well. Nothing is said at the time, but three of his lieutenants make a decision, a dangerous one that indicates their affection for David. They move through the Philistine lines—presumably under cover of darkness—fill a vessel from the well, make their way back to David, and present him with the water.

They get a surprising reception. David is astonished and deeply moved. He knows what could have happened. If they had been discovered, he would have been retrieving their corpses. Quite probably he reminds them of this brutal reality. He holds the vessel in his hands and is about to drink, but instead makes a decision. He announces that he will not drink.

Astonished, they wait for him to speak further. David again says that he will not drink, and this time gives his reason. The water, he maintains, is no longer merely water. It has been made sacred by the sacrifice that his three companions were willing to pay.

This is a moment of deep insight and deep sensitivity, and it tells us much about David as a human being. It also must have allowed David to see the depth of loyalty he was engendering in these tough men who had come into the hills with him. Moments such as this were to serve him well in the years to come, when David would be king. The friendships forged in these dangerous campaigns would translate into a formidable cadre of senior officers in David's army, fiercely loyal to him.

Leadership is many things and has many ingredients. Some exercise it by distancing themselves from those whom they see themselves as leading. Some work very hard at not revealing feelings that may hint at weakness or vulnerability. Some exercise leadership by inculcating fear, and some can be brutal in their treatment of others.

Where leadership is practised with wisdom—where it does not hesitate to communicate to others that their efforts are appreciated, their worth is realized, their humanity is affirmed—there will be ready response and mutual respect. Such leadership will be given cooperation and loyalty.

~ 7 ~

A Serious Commitment

I [Jeremiah] bought the field at Anathoth from my cousin Hanamel, and weighed out the money to him, seventeen shekels of silver. I signed the deed, sealed it, got witnesses, and weighed the money on scales. Then I took the sealed deed of purchase, containing the terms and conditions, and the open copy; and I gave the deed of purchase to Baruch ... in the presence of my cousin Hanamel, in the presence of the witnesses who signed the deed of purchase, and in the presence of all the Judeans who were sitting in the court of the guard. In their presence I charged Baruch, saying, Thus says the Lord of hosts, the God of Israel: Take these deeds ... and put them in an earthenware jar, in order that they may last for a long time. For thus says the Lord of hosts, the God of Israel: Houses and fields and vineyards shall again be bought in this land. Jeremiah 32:9–15

Suggested reading: Jeremiah 32:1–25

These days it is extraordinarily easy to live at a distance from real life. An extreme example is the pilot who releases the bomb from 10,000 feet and watches on a small screen for the flash that says the target has been obliterated. Less extreme is the senior bureaucrat who with one swift signature brings misery or prosperity to a whole community by depriving it of, or supplying it with, employment.

Even the social worker, physically near to a client family, must for professional reasons keep a distance, taking care not to become involved emotionally. And the now familiar world of e-mail can be at once linking yet distancing.

For years a doggedly courageous man played a thankless and even dangerous role in his city. His name was Jeremiah Ben Hilkiah, and he had unwillingly—because he entertained no illusions about it—accepted a deep inner call to be what his long-ago world called a prophet. Of all those in scripture to whom we give the name "prophet," none agonized more than Jeremiah about accepting the role.

We might think of the role of a prophet in Israel as being the moral conscience of society. Sometimes this entailed giving some news or opinion or judgement that was more than a little unwelcome. Add to this the fact that many prophets had to play out their role when the society was fearful and under stress. We can easily imagine how thankless Jeremiah's task was, especially since he lived at a time when his city lay under the approaching threat of the Babylonian empire.

For some years Jeremiah carries out his role faithfully as he sees it. God has called him—against every instinct in him— to prophesy. On many occasions he has pointed out the personal and systemic failures of his society. And he has repeatedly collided with its leaders. Even more annoying for his listeners, Jeremiah has had the gall to suggest that the Babylonian invaders are God's retribution for the injustice and corruption everywhere in Israel. This he has done with such power and incisiveness that his loyalty is being called into question and his life has begun to be threatened.

Jeremiah realizes the dilemma he faces. The more he speaks of Israel being justifiably punished, the less he will be listened to and the easier it will become to dismiss him as negative, self-defeatist, and even a traitor. Jeremiah knows that, unless he is heard and seen to be involved and committed to his people—which he most certainly is—he will become useless in his prophetic role. Even though in recent months he has taken great care to assure them that there will be a future of promise and possibility after the present disaster, they cannot hear this.

At this point Jeremiah does the most utterly unexpected thing. He buys a piece of land. To be precise, he buys a field in neighbouring Anathoth, a district near the city. Ironically, we can safely surmise that he got the land at a good price because it is highly probable that the very people who were loudly condemning him for being negative about the future were themselves rapidly turning their property into whatever cash they could lay their hands on.

Jeremiah deliberately made his purchase in a public manner. He made sure that all his critics heard of it. The message he was determined to send was obvious. No longer was he fulminating from the sidelines. He had become a hands-on participant in whatever fate confronted his country, and everyone could see that this fate was now very near.

Jeremiah's purchase and his announcement remind us of the moment when Jack Kennedy, as visiting United States president, climbed the wooden platform to look over the Berlin Wall in 1963 and said four very simple but immensely significant words: "Ich bin ein Berliner." Both of these actions, separated by many centuries, were a gesture of support that left no doubt in anyone's mind. Jeremiah had stepped from commentator to fully involved participant in whatever his country had to face. And to prove this, he had put himself on the line.

Only for so long can we remain outside of life. There comes a time when the physician must allow herself or himself to hear the fear and worry that no medication or procedure can remedy. When the priest must realize that the most beautiful liturgies cannot substitute for a pastoral ministry that walks closely with his or her people. When the politician must understand that the most brilliantly crafted image can never substitute for human presence. When a parent must discover that affluence and luxury provided to one's family can never substitute for caring and sometimes costly love.

As Jeremiah knew, life cannot be lived from the sidelines.

~ 8 ~

A Recipe for Survival

The end of all things is near; therefore be serious and discipline yourself for the sake of your prayers. Above all, maintain constant love for one another, for love covers a multitude of sins. Be hospitable to one another without complaining. Like good stewards of the manifold grace of God, serve one another with whatever gift each of you has received. Whoever speaks must do so as speaking the very words of God; whoever serves must do so with the strength that God supplies, so that God may be glorified in all things through Jesus Christ. To him belong the glory and the power forever and ever. Amen. 1 Peter 4:7–11

Suggested reading: 1 Peter 4:7–11

We live at a time when there is much concern about the many things that seem to be ending. This concern applies to almost every aspect of modern life. We may discover ourselves in a conversation about the possible ending of the family as a viable entity in society. We may find ourselves generally agreeing that in methods of education, and delivery of health care and social programs, an era is ending. We are unsure what will be the shape of such things in the future.

Beyond these concerns there is a whole literature of endings themes, including the millions of copies of the *Left Behind* series being sold, the popularity of blockbuster disaster movies, and the sordid scenarios whereby life on earth may come to an unpleasant end—some to do with viruses, or global warming, or meteorites colliding with the earth.

When Christian faith was still only a generation or two old, there was also a sense of living in an ending time. A source for this presentment was the destruction of the city of Jerusalem by the Roman army in AD 70 and the demolition of the Temple, the centre of Jewish faith and, to this point, of Christian worship. So sacred was this building to that generation of both Jews and Christians, that they felt widespread fear and saw in this desecration a sure sign of the ending of the world, as they knew it.

From time to time in the decades that followed, there were outbreaks of persecution of Christians. Roman society deeply distrusted religious beliefs other than the traditional Roman religious system. They feared the instability and the weakening of the social fabric that was sure to follow. Local persecutions could sometimes be cruel and demoralizing to the small local community.

Such experiences raised many questions for the early

Christian leaders. They had looked for an early return of their Lord. Now older members of the community were dying without seeing any such return. Questions abounded, particularly when it began to become costly and dangerous to hold the still new faith. There came even more questions, some of them desperate as people faced either torture or death. Many of these questions were directed to the leadership of the movement. Among that leadership was the now aging apostle Peter.

By this time the movement had spread widely, especially in western Asia Minor (part of today's Turkey). To these regions Peter circulates a letter. His obvious purpose is to encourage those who feel themselves under great pressure, even under threat of losing their lives for no reason other than being Christian.

It is interesting for us, many centuries later, to read Peter's words to that long-ago world—so unlike ours on the surface, but so very like ours in the changing relationship between Christian faith and Western culture. A faith that once permeated the culture is rapidly being repudiated and pushed to the margins of social and political life.

Peter begins bluntly: "The end of all things is near." But what comes after his opening words is tremendously valuable for us today. Ironically a great part of its value lies in the simplicity and downright ordinariness of what Peter prescribes for dangerous and stressful times.

"Be serious and discipline yourselves for the sake of your prayers." This is so far from our usual concept of prayer—often little more than routine or hurried requests for divine assistance. Instead, Peter affirms a discipline of prayer—a time, however short, when the mind and heart turn intentionally to a presence other than the million things going on around us.

"Above all, maintain constant love for one another, for love covers a multitude of sins." We make so many judgements. We so easily react to hurts, real or imagined. But we need at least a few relationships that are made of sterner stuff, where our commitment to one another is impervious to the ups and downs of feelings and reactions.

"Be hospitable to one another without complaining." In a largely impersonal and lonely society, there is nothing more strengthening than to know that you have friends with whom you can eat and drink and laugh and, sometimes, even weep—friends who know you and your home and your loved ones with an intimacy you reciprocate.

"Serve one another with whatever gift each of you has received ... do so with the strength that God supplies, so that God may be glorified in all things." There are so many levels to this admonition. Serve one another, thus avoiding the trap of a self-centred and therefore self-defeating life.

"With whatever gift each of you has received." Remember the importance, first of knowing one's own gifts, then of finding a cause or focus into which we wish to throw ourselves with a passion.

"The strength that God supplies." We need to be aware that there are spiritual resources beyond ourselves that we can draw upon. We are hearing from a giant of the Christian story how necessary he felt this awareness to be.

Here we have spiritual counsel so simply and straightforwardly expressed as to seem almost too simple for our own time's complexity. Yet these things named by Peter are neither simple nor complex, but profoundly true and timeless. To realize their importance is a recipe not only for survival in an ancient world, but for rich and balanced living in any period of history.

Accepting Responsibility

In Tolkien's great epic *Lord of the Rings,* there is a moment when Gandalf approaches Frodo the Hobbit with an immense challenge. The ring must be taken into the very heart of the evil Sauron's territory. Everything now depends on Frodo's decision. The whole future of the quest, even—within the story—the future of the world, hangs in the balance. Will Frodo accept Gandalf's call to be the ring bearer? Frodo agonizes about the decision, then answers, "I will take the ring, though I do not know the way."

What gives us the strength to accept great responsibility? Sometimes people will accept responsibility that they know is far beyond their strength, as they understand it at the time. Florence Nightingale wondered at her own acceptance of a task that more than once seemed to have become almost impossible.

We have said that, for Christian people, the source of inspiration is the Holy Spirit—a strength beyond themselves. The same is true for others who accept great responsibility. Countless men and women in positions of leadership have voiced their conviction that a strength other than their own enabled them to carry on.

Esther is a commoner who has found herself on the throne of the world's mightiest empire at that time. No sooner does she realize this than she learns that she stands in danger of losing everything. Yet the moral choice she faces—her own safety or that of her people—will not allow her to escape. She must decide to take on a terrible and dangerous responsibility. Choosing to carry out this responsibility, she finds herself given strength beyond her own.

Isaiah is just a young man when the pleasant world he has come to take for granted collapses. Until now, his life has been easy. He lives in the top echelon of society, and the king's son is his companion. Responsibility is the concern of the older generation. Suddenly the king dies, and Isaiah realizes that he and his circle must now shoulder great responsibility. Their country is in a parlous state. The world around them is threatening. At first Isaiah panics, but then he finds himself seeking the presence of God. In doing so, he too discovers a strength beyond his own.

From the moment of his dramatic and life-changing conversion, it was obvious that much of the task of developing the new faith would fall on Paul's shoulders. What hung in doubt for a short period was whether the community he had recently been trying to destroy would bring itself to trust him. Trust having been established, a huge burden then fell on his shoulders. Almost single-handedly he took the new faith out of the small local world envisioned by the apostles. In the letters he came to write, he tells again and again of his dependence on the risen Christ. Here, for Paul, is the source of his strength.

We don't know a great deal about Priscilla, but what we do know suggests an extraordinarily energetic woman. From the beginning of her embracing Christian faith along with her husband, Aquila, she shows herself ready to assume responsibility. Not only does she play the role of natural and almost instinctive evangelist, she also becomes a builder of congregations, seeding them through house churches. While Priscilla herself never tells us of the source of her ability to be responsible for so much, everything we know about her tells us that her strength is in Jesus, crucified and risen.

All of these people would echo Paul's statement: "I can do all things through [Christ] who strengthens me."

~ 9 ~

The Cost of Integrity

Now Esther was admired by all who saw her. When Esther was taken to King Ahasuerus in his royal palace in the tenth month, which is the month of Tebeth, in the seventh year of his reign, the king loved Esther more than all the other women ... so that he set the royal crown on her head and made her queen instead of Vashti. Esther 2:15–17

Suggested reading: Book of Esther

S ometimes when we come across someone who has been very successful in his or her personal life, we look for something more. We look to see if they have involved themselves in the life and welfare of others. If someone has become very prominent in public life, we tend to ask what commitments they are prepared to make, and what activities they are prepared to involve themselves in, other than those that are to their own advantage.

We are in a situation of dazzling power. The Persian empire is at its height. We are told of "one hundred twenty seven provinces from India to Ethiopia"—huge even by today's standards of empire. We know immediately we are among power brokers. At the centre of power is Ahasuerus, king in his capital of Susa.

A domestic crisis is developing. For a reason we are not told, Queen Vashti refuses her husband's summons. Immediately this is regarded as a threat to public law and order, for now all women in the empire will know that a wife may refuse attendance on her husband. Vashti is banished from the king's presence, and the search begins for a new queen.

Scattered throughout the empire is a large Jewish minority, represented for us by Mordecai. Mordecai has a very beautiful niece named Esther who attracts the attention of the king. Esther eventually becomes queen, lifted from obscurity to a position of immense influence.

It is at this point that her life becomes complicated by a real threat to her Jewish community. A dangerous and powerful member of the court, named Haman, is determined to institute a pogrom that will have tragic consequences. To read Haman's words to the king is to hear the chilling patterns of recurring anti-Semitism down the centuries, even to the euphemistic language that cloaks evil intent.

"There is a certain people scattered and separated among the peoples in all the provinces of your kingdom; their laws are different from those of every other people, and they do not keep the king's laws, so that it is not appropriate for the king to tolerate them." Only after this careful and nuanced statement is the real intention laid bare in much more brutal language. "If it pleases the king, let a decree be issued for their destruction." For reasons unknown, Ahasuerus agrees and begins a process that will lead to death for tens of thousands of people.

Mordechai desperately contacts Esther. Only she can get the king to rescind his proclamation. The request deeply distresses her. She has not revealed to Ahasuerus that she herself is of this threatened minority. Now she must risk losing everything that she has gained, or remain silent while her own people are destroyed.

Esther contacts Mordechai through a messenger. He points to Haman as the main instigator and sends Esther the document that condemns Jews to death. Esther's reply is full of anxiety and helplessness. She cannot go to the king unless he summons her. Mordechai's reply is stern and adamant. Again its language is chillingly modern, echoing many voices that spoke before and during Hitler's holocaust.

"Do not think that in the king's palace you will escape any more than all the other Jews. For if you keep silence at such a time as this, relief and deliverance will rise for the Jews from another quarter, but you and your father's family will perish." Then Mordechai unerringly pinpoints the heart of the matter. "Who knows? Perhaps you have come to royal dignity for just such a time as this."

This magnificently nuanced message, with its implied reference to Esther's own integrity, has the desired effect. Esther agrees to go to the king. She makes it quite clear that she has no illusions about the possible consequences. "I will go to the king, though it is against the law; and, if I perish, I perish."

Three days later she decides to make her move. Dressing in all the grandeur of her queenly robes, she takes up position in a gallery where the king is likely to see her. Her plan succeeds and she is called to Ahasuerus's presence. She does not immediately bring up the crucial subject of the pogrom. She invites the king and Haman to a meal. Haman, eager for any royal recognition, comes. Both again receive an invitation from the queen, this time for another banquet on the morrow. And both accept.

The moment comes in the banquet when Ahasuerus turns to Esther and asks what her request is. She makes the request but subtly ignores the king's proclamation and instead points to Haman's hatred and treachery as the real reason for this threat to her people. The diplomatic way she has made her request succeeds. The king hastily lifts the proclamation, sending couriers out across the empire. Haman is hanged. Mordechai is given the royal signet ring that gives him immense power in the royal court.

In this long-ago political struggle, and in the efforts of a people to survive, we are given a glimpse of a courageous woman making a momentous choice. After a very understandable struggle with her conscience, Esther accepts that she must put public duty above private gain, even above personal survival.

While it is easy to preach pieties about such things, the fact is that each one of us can, from time to time, find ourselves faced with choices that can be made with integrity only by considerable sacrifice. If we are prepared to take even a short time, to lay before God the choice we face, while the burden and the cost of our choosing may not be lifted, we will find a grace beyond our own strength.

～ 10 ～

A Presence
Beyond Panic

*In the year that King Uzziah died, I saw the Lord
sitting on a throne, high and lofty; and the hem of his
robe filled the temple. Seraphs ... called one to another and said: "Holy, holy, holy is the Lord of hosts;
the whole earth is full of his glory." The pivots on the
thresholds shook ... the house filled with smoke. And I
said: "Woe is me! I am lost, for I am a man of unclean lips, and I live among a people of unclean lips;
yet my eyes have seen the King, the Lord of hosts!"*
Isaiah 6:1–5

Suggested reading: Isaiah 6:1–13

We deal in different ways with the crises that arise in our lives. Sometimes we can be shattered, utterly incapable of grappling with the situation when left to our own pathetic devices. If we are fortunate, we will find support—perhaps for a long time—from faithful friendship, from those who most love us, or from professional help. Sometimes we find the strength to deal with what has been unthinkable in our life to this point.

Very often in our thirties, we find ourselves making big decisions—the second and more serious job, the commitment to marriage and the possibility of children, the growing realization that we live in a harsh and unpredictable world not necessarily devoted to our personal welfare. At this stage particularly, we can be vulnerable to the unexpected event that pitches us into crisis. Such patterns of human experience occur in every culture and every time in history.

We encounter Isaiah sometime in the seventh century BCE. His personal world is in turmoil, the world around him is threatening, his social world is fragile. To make things worse, he has suddenly found himself in the front line of responsibility. His friend, the king's son, has just brought news that his father has died. For both these young men, the carefree years of early manhood are suddenly over.

We are now given in scripture a vivid word picture of a person grappling with personal crisis and being forced to make significant decisions. What is described in the language of a past culture is a process essentially timeless. Most people, when they realize that they must think things through clearly, and that much depends on the decisions they are about to make, choose some place to be alone. For some it will be a walk on the seashore, for others a city park, for some a hilltop, for others the quietness of an open city church.

Isaiah chooses the latter. He goes to the temple in his city. There he tries to focus his mind on what is bedrock for him—the majesty and holiness of God, the ultimate reality that is beyond change or threat or transience. Standing before this ultimate resource, he then, and only then, allows the full force of his fears and his lostness to sweep over him. He acknowledges that his world is being shaken to its foundations.

Yet in this shaking Isaiah feels called. All he can tell at this point is that this call is to responsibility. He knows very well how he feels. But he does not yet know how to respond and act. One thing that remains clear in the shaking of his world is the conviction that he is being mysteriously called to serve in some as yet unknown way. Instinct tells him that the all-important thing is to cling to this conviction.

It is far from easy. It takes a supreme effort, because deep within him is the wish to reject any sense of call, to be free of the weight of responsibility. Reality seems too complex, its demand too heavy. Isaiah feels that he simply has not got what he knows it will take to accept public responsibility and leadership in his society. In his desperate exclamation, "I am lost!" there is more than a hint of panic.

He now finds himself swept emotionally from loss of confidence to renewed resolve. He feels as if something is reaching out to him from beyond himself. Resources from deep within him and yet greater than himself begin to reinforce his resolve. His world is still in turmoil. What has to be faced before he came into this quiet place still has to be faced. But slowly he realizes that he is now regaining the ability to face it. There has not been any facile magic solution, but the capacity to handle the situation is returning. Isaiah has experienced God's grace. Almost as if he is overhearing someone else's voice, he hears himself saying Yes to whatever is ahead.

Isaiah is neither the first nor the last gifted human being to experience a sudden crisis of self-confidence. Very often it is precisely the very gifted person who is most vulnerable. Today a host of reports and statistics co-relate creativity and ability with the possibility of depression and even panic attacks. Perhaps some of this arises from the fact that being gifted and creative gives us the luxury—should we say the illusion?—of being in charge of our lives to this point.

Suddenly we find ourselves confronted with something that we are most certainly not in charge of, something that is in fact very much in charge of us—a monster that refuses to go away and refuses to be ignored until we engage it and wrestle with it. Even when we get professional assistance, we realize that we ourselves must develop techniques and disciplines to help us face further attacks.

As we hear Isaiah being addressed by God, we are made aware of something borne out in the experience of many. Anyone who has been through deep depression or panic attacks will point to a moment when they realized that only a source of strength from beyond themselves can help. This realization—that one does not wrestle alone—has for many made all the difference.

~ 11 ~
A Welcoming Community

Saul, still breathing threats and murder against the disciples of the Lord, went to the high priest and asked him for letters to the synagogues at Damascus, so that if he found any who belonged to the Way, men or women, he might bring them bound to Jerusalem.

Acts 9:1–2

Suggested reading: Acts of the Apostles 9:1–19

Very few things are more frightening than realizing you are not in control of your life. We take such control for granted. Perhaps nowhere do we expect it more than in our physical faculties. Only when we feel the chilling suspicion that some part of us may be threatened—sight, hearing, sexuality, muscular dexterity—do we realize how much we depend on these things. If the feeling passes and the fear proves groundless, we experience a deep appreciation of our faculties.

The highway from Jerusalem to Damascus goes north along the Jordan valley, curves around the east side of the Lake of Galilee, then veers northeast into Syria and on to its capital city. One day in the year AD 36 we might have seen a small entourage heading toward the capital. There may have been three or four horses. Most probably one rider was leading.

As we watch, the lead horse comes to a sudden halt. The animal, seemingly startled, rears up, throwing its rider to the ground. Temporarily disoriented and obviously hurt, the fallen man calls out as if in conversation with another. His companions watch mesmerized while he slowly picks himself up and stands unsteadily looking around. Only then do they realize that he cannot see them. Saul is blind.

We have been present at one of the great moments in the story of Christian faith. We have watched Saul—a sworn enemy of the newborn faith—encounter on this highway what he will swear to the end of his life is the presence of the risen and living Christ. Again and again he will tell this experience. It will become the cornerstone of his self-understanding and all that happens subsequently in his life.

The event seems to have happened not many miles from Damascus. His companions lead Saul into the city, find lodgings, and—whether at his request we don't know—leave him alone. For three days he remains there in terrifying darkness. He must have been tempted to assume that his future life was shattered. He neither eats nor drinks. This powerful government official is completely immobilized. From time to time he sleeps. In his sleep there may have been a dream, certainly a desperate hope, of someone coming to give him back what he wants more than anything else in the world—his sight.

Not until the third day does he hear anything other than the sounds of the surrounding city. Now there are footsteps. A door opens, and the footsteps continue across the room toward him. It must have been a chilling moment. He may have braced himself for an attack, feeling helpless to prevent it. Then he feels a gentle hand on his shoulder, an equally gentle voice speaking two utterly unexpected words: "Brother Saul," then with deliberation and concern in every syllable, the voice continues, "the Lord Jesus, who appeared to you on your way here, has sent me so that you may regain your sight and be filled with the Holy Spirit."

For Saul, that moment must have been powerful and complex. Immediately there would have been a flood of relief that the unseen visitor was friend rather than enemy, and that he, Saul, was somehow being accepted rather than attacked. But the very sound of the name Jesus would also have brought back the nightmare moment on the Damascus highway when his carefully constructed life had disintegrated under a power far beyond his own.

What seemed an incredible dream is now for Saul a reality. His sight returning, he looks up at the face of Ananias. Within hours he is surrounded by the community he had come to destroy. Not long afterward they watch wonderingly—

some of them dubiously—as their most dreaded enemy accepts the water and the Spirit of Christian baptism.

Many things other than religious experience can suddenly send our lives into a tailspin, forcing us to reassess who we are and what our lives are about. But we see in the experience of Saul one very important thing. Not only was his life suddenly sent careering off the neat and predictable path he had so carefully constructed. The same force that caused this change became the foundation and inspiration for the rest of his life, so much so that he felt impelled to take a new name. From now on he would be Paul.

When we feel that life has been taken from our control, it makes a great difference if we can link with what we believe to be the very source of our lives. For a Christian this source is God, and the person through whom we are linked to God is Jesus. We say—sometimes saying it too easily and casually—we believe that Jesus is Emmanuel, God with us. If this is true, then God in Christ is with us even through the crisis in our lives that seems to take control from us.

As with Paul, so with us. The same Jesus asks for our trust in any great change in circumstances through which we are being taken. As countless other faithful men and women have discovered, Jesus offers a community of friendship that can draw us in. In this community we are offered a vision of the new person we have become, and we are called to serve in ways that will once again give our lives fulfillment and satisfaction.

~ 12 ~

A Lived Commitment

*After this Paul left Athens and went to Corinth.
There he found a Jew named Aquila, a native of
Pontus, who had recently come from Italy with his
wife Priscilla, because Claudius had ordered all Jews
to leave Rome. Paul went to see them, and, because
he was of the same trade, he stayed with them, and
they worked together—by trade they were
tentmakers....*

*After staying there for a considerable time, Paul said
farewell to the believers and sailed for Syria, accom-
panied by Priscilla and Aquila.... When they reached
Ephesus, he left them there.... Then he set sail from
Ephesus.* Acts 18:1–3; 18–21

Suggested reading: Acts of the Apostles 18
and 1 Corinthians 16:19

Even in lively Christian congregations there can be a great amount of passivity. Paradoxically, the better the quality of leadership, the greater this passivity may be. Many people may be involved, but only as a response to the initiative of others who are employed to create opportunities for Christian activities. It may be that, while this reactive activity is going on, those who lead the congregation are praying for signs of at least a small group of people who will themselves come forward with ideas for projects, and who will realize and act out a ministry that they recognize as their own.

In the year AD 49 the emperor Claudius made a decision that was to affect the lives of thousands of Jewish people living in Rome. He ordered them out of Italy. Among them was a well-travelled couple named Aquila and Priscilla. They had come to Rome from the province of Pontus in Asia Minor, where they were probably living on the lovely Black Sea coast.

These two people were tentmakers, whose skill and trade could make them very affluent. An indication of this is the discovery, not many years ago in England, of the record of a contract given by the Roman army to a firm of tentmakers, a contract for 42,000 tents! It is quite likely that Aquila and Priscilla had such contracts. When we look at the series of places we know they lived in—Pontus, Rome, Corinth, and Ephesus—we see that every one of these cities would have included a large Roman army garrison.

The couple moved to Corinth, little knowing that they were about to make the acquaintance of someone who would change their lives. Somewhere in Corinth the person we know as Paul was living. He too was a tentmaker, and it may have been through this shared occupation that the three of them got together. Eventually, under Paul's guidance, Aquila and Priscilla became Christians.

For about a year and a half they worked and prayed and studied together. This time was not without crisis, even real danger. After a very rough confrontation in the local synagogue, Paul made the far-reaching decision to take his newly found faith beyond the world of the synagogue.

Soon afterward, a much more concerted attack was made on Paul, dragging him before the Roman authorities of the city. The case was dismissed, but the community must have decided that Paul could not be useful in Corinth until some time had passed and tempers had cooled. With Aquila and Priscilla he set sail for Syria. Whether the subsequent stop in Ephesus was a change of mind we do not know. There they parted, Paul going on to Syria, his friends remaining in Ephesus, most probably to set themselves up once again as tentmakers.

At this point the couple shows how quickly they had grasped the fact that their baptism had called them into ministry. There appeared in the city a man named Apollos, a Jew from Alexandria, who had been formed by John the Baptist's religious movement. Aquila and Priscilla took him under their wing and instructed him more fully in the new Christian faith. So well did they do this that, when Paul returned to the city, he made Apollos leader of the local Christian community.

Here is a wonderful example of what today we would call lay ministry. These two people were close friends of the towering figure who was himself forming Christian communities in city after city, yet there is no sign that Aquila and Priscilla felt they should wait for Paul's direction or encouragement. They exercised their ministry to wonderful effect and brought into Christian fellowship a magnificent ally. In addition, they began gathering a small congregation in their home. Paul mentions them and their house church when he writes to the Christian community in Corinth.

Sometime later, in his letter to the Christian community in Rome, Paul mentions his friends again. There is a tantalizing hint that times had got rough for the three of them in Ephesus. Paul sends warm greetings to Aquila and Priscilla for "risking their necks for my life." Apart from anything else, this greeting in his letter suggests that the couple had returned to Rome when the emperor's ban against Jews had been lifted. Paul adds a significant sentence. He says, "Aquila and Prisca, together with the church in their house, greet you warmly." Once again, as they had already done in Ephesus, this couple has shown their readiness to take initiative and to exercise their ministry.

There is an attractiveness and energy that comes across time to us from Aquila and Priscilla. Six times they are mentioned in the New Testament record and—interesting and unusual in that culture—in four of these references Priscilla is mentioned first. Paul, who is not given to easy intimacies, even has a nickname for her. He calls her Prisca.

One such couple in a congregation, in any organization, can make an immense difference. Half a dozen, and anything is possible. Yet we need to remind ourselves that such exercising of ministry is exactly what baptism calls us to. There is a prayer for baptismal candidates: "Lord, fill them with your holy and life giving Spirit.... Teach them to love others in the power of the Spirit.... Send them into the world in witness to your love." These words may not have been said on the occasion of Aquila's and Priscilla's baptism, but they certainly went out and lived them.

Struggling With Our Humanity

Recently I was tidying books on my study shelves—a never-ending necessity—and I found myself holding a Penguin edition of *The Epic of Gilgamesh*. It is probably the oldest story in all literature, discovered in the Euphrates delta in the nineteenth century, but estimated to have originated at least fifteen hundred years before Homer. The epic is extraordinary for its timelessness. Gilgamesh, chastened by the sudden death of his dearest friend Enkidu, finds himself lonely, anxious, even fearful. He sets out on a quest to discover the meaning of death and life, thereby searching for the meaning of his own life.

The list of those who struggle to understand their own humanity is long and most certainly includes each of our names. We continually wrestle with the shadowed parts of our lives—our fears, angers, anxieties, and the limits that these feelings put on our ability to live life fully. From the moment that Eve and Adam leave the garden in the first pages of scripture, this struggle with our own humanity begins. In various forms it continues throughout the biblical record.

Towering over almost every other figure in the Old Testament is that of Abraham. Desert warrior, leader of a tribe, founder of a people, patriarch in all three of the great religions of the Middle East, a more formidable and awe-inspiring character is difficult to imagine. Yet on more than one occasion scripture does not hesitate to show us Abraham struggling with being Abraham! On these occasions this great human being has no illusions that he can carry out his vocation alone. He must, and does, turn to God.

On the surface Jacob is a success story. He is successful in love and certainly in business. We could even say that he has successfully built a life after a most unpromising beginning. But in later years we begin to get hints of how costly this success has been. We see him here wrestling with self-evaluation. Is he merely the material wealth he has accumulated, or is he more? This is scripture's way—God's way—of telling us about our own wrestling with who we are, who we wish to be, and the price we are prepared to pay for being changed.

There is a peculiar irony in the moment when we see the boy Samuel and the old high priest Eli standing together outside the doors of their people's place of worship. The old man has known great public power, but he has been humbled by failures in his own personality and his family life. In a strange repetition, Samuel will know similar experiences as an adult and as an old man. He too will wield great public power, but will show himself to be limited in his ability to accept and direct change in his society. He too will be shamed and humiliated by the behaviour of his family.

No public role, however well or successfully carried out, frees us from the inner struggles of personal life. If we are prepared to ask for God's help in our struggling, we will be given a grace that will also serve us in carrying out our public responsibilities.

～ 13 ～

A Walk in Darkness

As the sun was going down, a deep sleep fell upon Abram, and a deep and terrifying darkness descended upon him.... On that day the Lord made a covenant with Abram, saying, "To your descendants I give this land, from the river of Egypt to the great river, the river Euphrates." Genesis 15:12–18

Suggested reading: Genesis 15

In every age people have been afflicted by depression. There are countless expressions of it down through time—from medieval scribes, classical writers, romantic poets, to modern voices.

In our own day we have various techniques and disciplines for treating depression. Some turn to prayer and meditation as a resource. Many keep functioning by chemical means. Sometimes depression can balloon into panic. Recent statistics tell us that drugs used for panic attacks may be the most frequently prescribed pharmaceuticals in medical practice.

It would be strange if such a common human experience were not reflected in scripture. Ironically we discover depression in the life of one of the Bible's greatest figures. While Abram is far from young, he is still in the early stage of his desert wanderings, and he has found that such wanderings take him into some very dangerous places.

When we meet him in this scripture, he has just survived a significant threat. He has more than proved his mettle before certain rival tribes and their leaders. From now on, he has the satisfaction of knowing that he and his extended family will not only be treated with respect—they will be feared. And this fear will provide even more security for the future. It is at this juncture—when Abram must have been feeling a sense of achievement—that the shadow descends.

In the desert the silence of night can be almost a palpable reality. Such silence is far more than the absence of sound—it is a presence. With darkness as its ally, silence can have a profound effect on our thoughts. Perhaps the most insidious weapon of depression is its ability to search out what we are worried about but have previously managed to counter or suppress in our daytime activities. Who among us has not known such troubling times, whether or not we name God as our companion in the dialogue?

During Abram's dialogue with God in the night hours, the first words that sound in his mind are "do not be afraid." Immediately we know that the shadow is descending on Abram, and a moment later we hear him put his fear into words. "O Lord God, what will you give me, for I continue childless?" This may not be our own particular or current fear, but as we know, human fears are various and plentiful and can assail us any time.

The moment Abram's fear is put into words, it gets larger. His anxiety level rises as he says, "You have given me no off-spring, and so a slave ... is to be my heir!" Panic is surfacing.

A night encounter with anxiety can swing us from fear to confidence and back again. Abram hears himself addressed, this time reassuringly. "No one but your very own issue shall be your heir." For a moment Abram is reassured. But then he becomes restless—as we all can do in the small hours. Abram gets up and goes outside. The stars blaze in the desert sky. Their very number speaks to him of possible descendants. For a moment Abram relaxes. "He believed the Lord."

Wisely Abram searches for reassuring thoughts within himself. He realizes how far he has come. This land is now his. He understands this achievement as God's gift to him. "I am the Lord who brought you from Ur ... to give you this land to possess." But no sooner is this thought voiced than fear returns. True, he may have this land now, but can he keep it? Might he not lose everything? He has had numerous lessons in the brutality and unpredictability of his world. He voices a frantic plea for guarantees. "How am I to know that I shall possess it?"

What follows would have taken time and not a little preparation, and is unlikely to have happened immediately. Perhaps sleep came with the resolve to do something when day dawned. Abram decides to deal with his fears by ritual. Even in our own secularized world, we have rituals for dealing with our fears. We have learned that performing certain actions or focusing our thoughts in certain ways help us to deal with fear. We get a sense of being in communication with forces that we feel and know to be unimaginably stronger than ourselves.

These devices may succeed for us, but there may also be times when fear overwhelms us, and we realize that we must let fear work its will with us, until it passes. We read that "a deep and terrifying darkness descended upon [Abram]." The very doing of the ritual makes Abram realize that he is not in control. God is in control, and Abram must bow his head before this reality. We see how, in the darkness, he realizes that there is no easy solution. There will be a long struggle. Only when he accepts this fact, and bows before it, is he able to feel himself once again in covenant with a loving God.

All of us know such dark episodes. We know those times when we cannot manage by ourselves. We know the alternating bouts of confidence and terror that grip us. We know the nights when we have to bow before the shadow and let it, at least for a while, have its way with us, sweeping over us like a great wave. And somewhere in that experience of being swept along by something immeasurably more powerful than anything we can bring to bear, we find ourselves experiencing a sense of peace. Some are prepared to name this peace as the presence of a loving God.

～ 14 ～

Realizing Self-Worth

[Jacob] took a present for his brother Esau.... These he delivered into the hand of his servants, every drove by itself, and said to his servants, "Pass on ahead of me, and put a space between drove and drove." He instructed the foremost, "When Esau my brother meets you and asks you, 'To whom do you belong? Where are you going? And whose are these ahead of you?' then you shall say, 'They belong to your servant Jacob; they are a present sent to my lord Esau.' "

Genesis 32:13–18

Suggested reading: Genesis 32:13–21

In our culture contentment is an elusive quality. One reason is that we have entire industries and professions with the sole purpose of preventing us from being content. Our discontent—especially with what we do or do not have—is their business. Symptoms of this business are the various terms that have become so ubiquitous that we no longer notice them.

We hardly notice that almost everything is now a "product." There was a time when a bicycle or car was a product, and a number of less tangible things were called services. Today almost everything that requires any form of transaction is a product. It can be a particular aspect of banking. It can even be a medical procedure. But it is a product.

It is tempting to think that there was once a simpler world where such empty materialism did not obtain. But alas, it has always been the case that people's identity has been tied up more with what they have than with who they are.

For about thirty years Jacob, son of Isaac, brother of Esau, has been running away. During those years he has become powerful and affluent, and his extended family a force to reckon with. He has been running from his brother Esau, whom he swindled very early in their lives, and from whom he had to run, thinking that he would be attacked, perhaps even killed.

Running away has a law of diminishing returns. We simply tire of flight. It comes to dominate our thinking and to shape our life. Very often there comes a moment when we turn for home, whatever the consequences. We encounter Jacob at this precise point in his life. What he now does is very interesting as an essay in our human nature.

We do not know why Jacob decides at this stage that he must meet his brother. But that is his purpose. He is moving south with what we would consider his business empire. The instruments of that empire are largely animals and slaves. Jacob has massive flocks of sheep, goats, and camels. In his world these, as well as human beings, are currency.

His messengers tell him that his brother is coming north. They add the ominous news that he has four hundred men with him. For a moment all Jacob's fears surface. He must have known the temptation to turn tail and flee. But he fights his fear, probably because he realizes that he has become its prisoner, and this disgusts him.

Jacob's next actions tell us a great deal about his thinking, particularly about the values that have guided him to this point. He knows he has very little time. He uses that time to direct his men to divide everything into a series of separate caravans. We know there were at least three of these. A horde of animals and slaves are sent south to intersect with Esau's progress. The herdsman who leads has precise directions.

When Esau asks to whom this vast caravan belongs, the herdsman is to say that his master Jacob follows close behind. Not only that, but if Esau so wishes, he may consider all this wealth a present! If all goes according to Jacob's plan, this will happen at least three times. We do not even have to guess at the reason for this show of wealth. Jacob himself tells us. Speaking of his brother he says, "I may appease him with the present that goes ahead of me, and afterwards I shall see his face; perhaps he will accept me."

The long-ago storyteller is astute in his grasp of human nature. He remarks rather dryly, "So the present passed on ahead of him." There is a hint that what Jacob has become is actually more important than who he is, and this is quite true. The only way he can compensate is by a massive display of his accumulated possessions.

When the two brothers meet, a final irony is played out. Esau could not be less impressed by the clumsy display of wealth, nor does he need any part of it! We get the impression that he is actually rather amused. At his reaction, Jacob, while immensely relieved, is quite non-plussed!

The story is ancient; its theme is timeless. The theme is particularly suitable to our own time—an age of unequal but tremendous affluence, in which one individual can accumulate extraordinarily large amounts of wealth. As always, we need to be careful not to assume that such wealth is necessarily wrong.

When our Lord related the parable of the one who had accumulated great riches, he did not condemn those riches in themselves. Jesus' condemnation was directed only to the expressed attitude of the owner to his wealth. "I will say to my soul, 'Soul, you have ample goods laid up for many years; relax, eat, drink, be merry.'" Our Lord's dismissal of this attitude is extraordinarily harsh.

Jacob was fortunate because he came to realize the dubious value of possessions through the affectionate and bemused response of his brother. We are fortunate when we understand that our true worth lies not in what we may or may not have accumulated, but in who we are.

～ 15 ～

A Grace Beyond Failure

*Now the boy Samuel was ministering to the Lord
under Eli. The word of the Lord was rare in those
days; visions were not widespread.*

*At that time Eli, whose eyesight had begun to grow
dim so that he could not see, was lying down in his
room; the lamp of God had not yet gone out, and
Samuel was lying down in the temple of the Lord,
where the ark of God was. Then the Lord called,
"Samuel! Samuel!" and he said, "Here I am!" and
ran to Eli, and said, "Here I am, for you called me."
But [Eli] said, "I did not call."* 1 Samuel 3:1–5

Suggested reading: 1 Samuel 3:1–18

One of the ultimate tests of our human fortitude can be the fear that our life has essentially been a failure, at least by the measurements we have chosen to apply to it. We are fortunate if this realization comes at a point when there are some years and energy left, either to recover what has been lost or to make changes in our life that may give us some good years. If the sense of abject failure—with its attendant feelings of depression and regret—comes near the end of life, we face a fearful challenge. And if we do not have any source of grace beyond ourselves we can indeed be lost.

In this incident in the life of Eli, we are given a searing portrait of such an experience. For many years Eli has been high priest, a position of great trust and influence. When we meet him, he is struggling with the realization that a career, which began with great hopes and considerable ability, is now shattered. In recent years he has begun to lose his grip. To make matters worse, his two sons have shamed the family by their behaviour, and made their father a figure of contempt for his inability to curb them.

They are now a byword in the country for the immorality of their lives. It is quite probable that the profligacy of his sons, more than anything else, has broken their father's spirit. As if this were not enough, he has been harshly confronted for his overall failure. He has been told in the bluntest of terms that there are those who think God has rejected him.

When we encounter Eli, he is fast asleep in his chamber in the place of worship at Shiloh. In another part of the building a youth is sleeping. His name is Samuel. He assists the old man with the chores and duties of the shrine. We are present at a moment that is about to change their lives, their relationship, and the course of Israel's history.

The boy is wakened by a sense of being summoned. He has heard his name spoken. Assuming the old priest is calling, Samuel runs to him. Eli wakes and denies that he has called. Samuel returns to his room. Again he hears his name, and again he goes to the only source he can think of for such a call. But again the old man wakes and assures Samuel that he did not call him.

Puzzled, perhaps fearful, Samuel returns to his bed and sleeps for a while, only to wake a third time, certain that he has heard his name. Probably hesitating before once again waking Eli, he finally enters the old man's presence. This time the response is different.

Eli, with the wisdom of long years, realizes that something of great significance is happening. Gently he instructs Samuel to go back, lie down, wait to hear the mysterious summons, and to respond with the words, "Speak, Lord, for your servant is listening." The boy does this, and the response he receives is chilling. Somehow, in the silence of the pre-dawn hours, Samuel is made aware of the retribution that awaits his elderly mentor.

Dawn breaks, and Samuel must encounter Eli as he opens the great doors for the day's duties in the shrine. Samuel tries to avoid the old man, but Eli will not be denied. He insists on being told what Samuel has learned. Against his will Samuel tells Eli the awful news of God's displeasure. At this moment Eli shows what a magnificent human being he is still capable of being. There is not a word of self-justification or self-pity. He acknowledges the justice of the verdict.

In due time the dreaded consequences of the old man's failed policies appear. The unthinkable happens. The sacred ark is lost to enemies. Eli's two sons are killed. When he hears the news, it is too much. Eli suffers a seizure and dies.

The story is unrelentingly tragic, or so it seems. There is, however, a redeeming moment when hope and meaning shine out. It comes in Eli's response to Samuel's dreadful news that God has rejected him and his family. Samuel listens, hears the boy out, then quietly says, "It is the Lord; let him do what seems good to him."

There are times in life when it seems that all has been lost, that everything we have given our lives to building has been demolished. We may even see clearly how and why things have happened as they have. Yet if there exists at the core of our being a sense that our lives are held in the hands of a loving God, then all need not be lost. There are many lives that will attest to this possibility of grace.

Eli's vision of God was one in which he had been summarily rejected. But in the vision of God given to us in Jesus Christ, we have a promise. Among the places it appears is in the letter to Hebrew Christians. "[God] has said, 'I will never leave you or forsake you.' So we can say with confidence, 'The Lord is my helper; I will not be afraid.' "

Moments of Self-Discovery

When we think about the phrase "to come to oneself," it seems a strange expression. How can one come to one-self? Surely we are always ourselves, always one with this strange and mysterious "I" who bears our name and occupies our body.

Yet it is indeed possible to meet this "I" in very unexpected and salutary ways. Suddenly it is almost as if we are outside ourselves looking in and realizing something about ourselves in a way we have never before experienced. Depending on the nature of such a moment we can know exhilaration, surprise, even joy. We have achieved something we did not think within our capability, or we realize that, against all our expectation, somebody really does love us. On the other hand a moment of coming to oneself can be very salutary.

The youth we know as the prodigal son has had a good time. Money has been plentiful; fair-weather friends have been in abundance. Suddenly it's all over. No more good times. In fact, very tough times. At this point something happens that speaks volumes for the kind of man he is deep down. He doesn't wallow in self-pity. He sees himself for the first time as he really is—warts and all. He comes to himself. It is a wonderful and grace-filled moment, and his response to it will make all the difference.

David the king comes to himself in a very different way. We might say that he is brought to himself in spite of himself. It is almost as if someone suddenly held up a mirror in which David sees his real self. What he sees appalls him. It's not as if he is unacquainted with what he sees in the mirror, but Nathan the prophet has removed the scales of self-deception from David's eyes and forced him to see more clearly and deeply.

Jacob also has help to see himself in a new way, help he most certainly does not want! It comes to him in the form of his brother Esau. For years Jacob has dreaded this encounter, but it cannot be avoided any longer. When they do at last meet, Jacob discovers something of which he has been unaware. He discovers that all these years he has been projecting an utterly unreal, even false, persona on to his brother. Esau has loomed in Jacob's thoughts as powerful, fierce, threatening, and vengeful. But the brother whom he meets is none of these things. Jacob realizes that the attributes he has projected on to Esau come from his own regrets and guilt, and are utterly mistaken. Jacob sees himself for the first time as having carried a burden for which there was no necessity.

Instances of coming to ourselves can be gifts of God. Many people in scripture are given such moments, and so are we. Pray that we recognize the gift when it is given, especially if it is a gift we are not sure we want to accept!

～ 16 ～

A Turning for Home

There was a man who had two sons. The younger of them said to his father, "Father, give me the share of the property that will belong to me." So he divided his property between them. A few days later the younger son gathered all that he had and travelled to a distant country. Luke 15:11–13

Suggested reading: Luke 15:11–32

M oments of self-revelation are mysterious. They can break into our lives any time, and sometimes in the most unlikely circumstances. It may be something said to us by a friend, something noticed in a book we are reading, something realized in a moment of introspection when our thought may be seemingly far removed from ourselves and our concerns.

When such moments do come, they are surprising, yet maybe not as surprising as they seem. When we have recovered from our initial shock, we may realize that our new self-awareness has been on the edge of our consciousness for some time. Now, all of a sudden, it has entered our experience front and centre, insisting on our attention.

Perhaps the most famous of such moments, certainly the most famous in Holy Scripture, is when the young man we know as the prodigal son "came to himself," realizing how foolish his behaviour had been and resolving to do something about it. The prodigal son has long been regarded as the classic reprobate who comes to his senses. The image of him creeping home to the arms of his welcoming and forgiving father has intrigued readers and hearers for generations. The tale has become universal, and the phrase "the prodigal son" has moved far beyond the bounds of scripture.

A father has two sons. The younger decides to leave home and so asks for his part of the inheritance. He eventually wastes everything and ends up in squalor. At this point he comes to himself, realizes his stupidity, and returns home full of abject apology, offering promises of good behaviour. To his astonishment neither is necessary. His father receives, forgives, and celebrates ecstatically.

But there is another character in this story—an older brother. He is upright and faithful, the soul of rectitude. He sees himself as having asked for nothing and as having received nothing. When his sibling returns and is feted for doing so, the elder brother is appalled and outraged. It would seem that the father has regained one son and lost another. While one has left and returned, the other seems to have "left" in a deeper sense.

The New Revised Standard Version of the Bible gives us an interesting hint of the significance of the elder brother by calling this chapter in the gospel, "The Parable of the Prodigal and his Brother." This seems to suggest that the two sons are much more bound up together than our telling of the story has tended to emphasize in the past.

For instance, it is easy to miss the fact that, when the younger son asks for his share, the father actually divides his property between the two. Presumably the older brother receives his share and becomes just as capable of deciding to leave home as his younger sibling. This fact points to an untruth in the older son's outburst, "you have never given me even a young goat!"

Younger siblings can have a problem establishing their own identity. It is possible that the actual moment when the prodigal comes to himself, or at least begins to come to himself, is in the act of asking for his share and leaving. In this he realizes that, to become himself, he must escape from the long shadows of both his elder brother and his father. The fact that he makes foolish subsequent decisions is almost beside the point. He has already made an extremely wise decision, and the consequences of his foolishness could be considered the necessary price of wisdom gained.

When eventually the prodigal son stands in the midst of squalor and the full enormity of his stupidity strikes him, the process of coming to himself is complete and the process of his homecoming begins. By contrast, it may be extremely difficult for the older brother to experience this process of coming to himself, because he has been under the illusion that he has always been fully in command of himself.

What of the relationship of the returned son and his father? Is the father sent on that wild run toward his son because he only now realizes that he has never before celebrated either of his sons, never given what every son or daughter needs and longs for—parental blessing? Does the father also come to himself?

When the father cries out that the lost has been found and the dead is alive, we might ask if something lost within himself has been found, if something dead within himself has come alive. There are times when the only way for a son or daughter to bring about parental change and receive such a blessing—which can also be a blessing for the parent—is to begin the process by rejection and escape.

Of all the parables of our Lord, this parable is brimming over with irony and subtlety in what it tells us about human character. Jesus seems to be saying that to come home we first have to leave home, to say Yes to life and to ourselves we first have to say No, to be found we first have to be lost. As we see too with the father, sometimes something has to be lost before it can be found.

Christian experience is replete with those who decide to run from a sense of an imprisoning God, only to find themselves turning for home and the arms of a God whom they realize is loving and liberating.

～ 17 ～
An Acknowledgement of Guilt

The thing that David had done displeased the Lord, and the Lord sent Nathan to David. He came to him, and said to him, "There were two men in a certain city, the once rich and the other poor.... [The rich man] took the poor man's lamb....

Then David's anger was greatly kindled against the man. He said to Nathan, "As the Lord lives, the man who has done this deserves to die; he shall restore the lamb fourfold, because he did this thing, and because he had no pity."

Nathan said to David, "You are the man!"

2 Samuel 12:1–7

Suggested reading: 2 Samuel 12:1–15

In recent years we have had numerous examples of the inability of people in high places to accept responsibility for their actions. This has been particularly obvious in the area of high finance and political life. More than one huge financial conglomerate has given us vivid images of its senior executives protesting their innocence about policies and actions in which it is almost inconceivable that they did not have firsthand information and full involvement.

At other times we have seen such executives desperately shifting responsibility on to others in an attempt to escape dire consequences. We have seen the spectacle in political life of fervent denials of sexual involvements that have subsequently turned out to be quite true. Accepting responsibility for our decisions and actions can sometimes be an agonizing challenge. There is a moment in scripture when we see this being played out at the highest level in a long-ago society.

It is early years for David as king in Israel. He has performed magnificently. Battles have been won, Jerusalem has been made a capital, various factions have been brought together. David is at the height of his popularity. It is well known that great success or fame can bring with it the sense of being beyond the rules that ordinary people must live by.

Perhaps this is precisely why David suddenly does something incredibly foolish and out of character—at least, to the extent that we know him to this point. He indulges in an affair with the young attractive wife of one of his senior army officers, ironically an officer who is utterly loyal to David. To compound the situation, when he realizes that Bathsheba is pregnant, David conspires in a particularly treacherous way to have her husband killed.

In a small and intimate society, such things cannot go unknown. It is unlikely that anyone would dare say anything to David, although, before he gets involved in the affair, he is warned that this young woman is not only an officer's wife but also the daughter of a prominent figure in the citadel. It is a measure of his infatuation—and, perhaps, of his arrogance—that David goes ahead with the affair.

Time passes—we are not sure how long. We do know that it was less than nine months because what now happens takes place before the birth of the child that is about to be born from the liaison. By now David has made Bathsheba his wife. Presumably the king assumes that tracks have been covered and, with any luck, memories are short. Even if there is trouble ahead, perhaps in the form of blackmail, it will likely be possible to deal with it by the judicious use of kingly favours. The world of political survival changes little down the centuries!

David does not yet know it, but he is about to be confronted by someone who cannot be silenced by royal favours. One day, while performing his role as judge, David is busily engaged with a succession of cases. Giving his verdict in a case, he gestures for the next plaintiff to come forward.

David was probably aware of Nathan's standing among the people as a person of immense integrity and even holiness, but judging from what now takes place, it is possible that the king did not know the prophet by sight. As David listens, what seems merely another citizen's plea to the king slowly becomes a tale of unscrupulous greed.

As Nathan tells it, a rich man has cruelly robbed a poor man. David is full of indignation. Falling directly into Nathan's trap, he demands to know the name of the perpetrator. In words that ring down through time Nathan says simply, "You are the man." There follows from Nathan a scathing condemnation of David's recent behaviour. Every ghastly detail is spelled out for public consumption.

It must have taken great courage. In that long-ago society the king's word was law. David could have had Nathan disposed of on the spot. There must have been a moment of dead silence. We will never know what went quickly through David's mind, but we do know his decision. In six short words he bowed his royal head before the moral power of Nathan's accusation. The words must have astonished all who heard them. With stark simplicity David said, "I have sinned against the Lord."

It is a defining moment in David's reign. Possibly it is an indication of something in his character for which people loved him and forgave him much. There is no effort to weasel out of the situation, no searching for excuses, no attempt to shift the blame on to Bathsheba. David accepts full responsibility for his actions. The readiness to do this without hesitation will become part of the totality of the man and of the king. In spite of his humanity—perhaps precisely because of it—he will retain the respect and affection of his people.

David's acknowledgement of guilt, and the way he states it, says much to us in a secular modern culture. He did not merely say, "I have sinned"—in itself a courageous statement of fact. He said, "I have sinned against the Lord." In our terms David assumed an absolute moral standard beyond his own subjective judgement, a standard by which his and all our actions are measured and judged. Ironically, it is only if we possess such a measurement, grounded in the reality we call God, that we can receive forgiveness other than our own sometimes self-indulgent acceptance and understanding.

～ 18 ～
An Unnecessary Burden

Now Jacob looked up and saw Esau coming, and four hundred men with him.... He himself went on ahead ... bowing himself to the ground seven times, until he came near his brother. But Esau ran to meet him, and embraced him, and fell on his neck and kissed him, and they wept....

Esau said, "What do you mean by all this company that I met?" Jacob answered, "To find favour with my lord." But Esau said, "I have enough, my brother; keep what you have for yourself." Jacob said, "No, please; if I find favour with you, then accept my present from my hand; for truly to see your face is like seeing the face of God."... So he urged him, and he took it. Genesis 33:1–11

Suggested reading: Genesis 33:1–11

The psychological phenomenon we call "projection" has become so well known, that it remains quite extraordinary how much projecting we go on doing in our everyday relationships. We are for ever making assumptions about how we are regarded by someone else, or how someone we know—or think we know—will behave under certain circumstances, or what somebody meant when they said something to us, or what motivation they had for something they have done. On we go with our projections in spite of their being so often mistaken.

Jacob and Esau are brothers, twins, but they have always been different from the very beginning of their lives. At the time of this incident they have not met for decades. Their only memories of one another are those of a disastrous childhood and youth and, if truth be told, of a very manipulative mother. An early experience has shaped the rest of the life for one of them. But that is now all in the past. The only problem is that those past events are very much part of the present!

These twins are utterly different. Jacob is a calculating, self-centred introvert. Esau is a hearty, generous, extrovert. Jacob has an eye for details and how they can be exploited for his benefit. Esau reaches out to life's possibilities, wanting only to discover them and live them all, even if it means paying a price. In their youthful years Jacob betrays Esau. It matters not how or for what. All we need to know is that, because of this betrayal, Jacob has had to leave home precipitously to avoid his brother's rage.

From this point on we come to know a great deal about Jacob and almost nothing about Esau. One goes north into lush grasslands, the other goes south into the desert. What we come to know about Jacob is for the most part far from attractive. We see a pattern developing, one that begins in youth and continues consistently as time goes by. Jacob hones to a fine art his ability to use and manipulate others. For some years he benefits by the example of an uncle who has prospered by displaying the same abilities as his nephew, but who eventually finds himself outmaneuvered by the nephew he must finally acknowledge as a superior rogue.

All through the years of increasing success and affluence, another reality has remained consistent in Jacob. He has always been haunted by the memory of those early days with Esau. He has heard about Esau from time to time, and what he has heard has not been reassuring. Esau has become a tribal leader to be reckoned with, and the last thing Jacob wishes is a reckoning, even though he himself has become formidable and powerful. He has acquired a carefully—and unscrupulously—built business empire.

But most of all Jacob wishes to keep his distance from Esau, because of the unrelenting guilt he feels about his long-ago betrayal of his brother. Of course he also believes that, without a shadow of a doubt, his brother hates and detests him and seeks revenge. How else could Esau possibly feel? So goes Jacob's logic, the kind of logic that has helped us all to make utterly mistaken projections about other people.

The occasion of their encounter is one of the most human—both amusing and pathetic—in the Bible. To his astonishment—and probably to his profound relief—Jacob finds that he is absolutely mistaken about this brother, whose anger he has dreaded for half a lifetime. To rub salt into the wound, Esau seems more than a little amused at his brother's discomfort. In fact, Esau appears to detect a certain nervousness in his brother. For his part, Jacob realizes that he has been projecting on to Esau feelings and attitudes that exist only in his own fevered and self-centred imagination.

The trouble with our projecting on to others is that we get caught in a wonderfully ironic circle. Most often we project onto the other what would be our own feelings and responses given the circumstances. In the same circumstances, we would feel resentful, angry, and aggrieved, so we assume that they must feel these things—and we can be so tragically wrong.

The other tragic thing about projections is that they tend to harden with the passing of time, so that it can seem impossible to do anything to rescue the situation. One of the most poignant moments in some relationships is when two people, estranged for years, have in some way been brought together by life, and one says, or maybe both hear themselves saying, "But I always thought that you ...."

Sometimes, by God's grace, such a sad moment can be transformed when we come to realize that long ago we were graciously forgiven the guilt that we assumed we had to carry.

Acknowledging Our Flaws

In its greatness Shakespearian tragedy presents us with a larger-than-life heroic character who, we gradually come to realize, is deeply flawed. When we first meet people like Macbeth or Othello, we see strength, self-confidence, command of self and others. But we also come to see the slow emergence of a crack or flaw in this carefully cultivated exterior, and we watch with something approaching horror, certainly deep dismay, as a single weakness brings the whole edifice crashing to the ground.

Although this is the stuff of high drama, something similar takes place in every human relationship. We discover someone, and we think they are wonderful. Years later we still love them, fully aware that they are not quite as wonderful—at least not in the way we first thought. They discover the same about us. To be human is to be flawed.

The Bible does not hesitate to let us see the flaws in the characters who walk its vast stage. One can almost say that the greater the figure, the more certainly we will be shown his or her feet of clay.

To meet Pontius Pilate, sixth procurator of Judea, personal emissary of the emperor, we would certainly have been very impressed. Here is a man who has clawed his way up the ladder of Roman governance. He has power to execute or to let live. He is married to one of the most powerful families in the empire. Impressive indeed. Yet almost immediately we begin to see weakness. If we look beyond scripture into the writings of Josephus, we see example after example of Pilate's weakness. In the trial that is to give Pilate's name an awful immortality, scripture will show us a weak and vulnerable official being manipulated with ease by some around him.

Our insight into Paul's character comes very differently. We know him as driven, single-minded, unyielding, certainly to himself and those who work with him. Now we listen as he speaks to a group of Christians going through a difficult time. Things are not in good shape in the Christian community in Corinth. We hear Paul outlining the spiritual gifts he wishes them to display. Now he begins to reflect about the greatest gift—love. As he does so, we realize something intriguing. Are we seeing a great figure expressing regret for a quality missing from his own life?

Saul, the young man we first encounter hiding, emerges reluctantly to accept anointing as king. We watch as he becomes king, giving every promise of fulfilling Samuel's expectations. Saul is larger than life physically and, in early years, in the exercising of his many gifts. But as we watch, we see the picture change. Cracks begin to appear in the powerful facade. Self-confidence is overtaken by fears, jealousies, sudden anger. Saul gradually loses the ability to relate to his mentor Samuel, his daughter Michal, his protegé David. We watch him at the last, broken and pathetic, crouching in a cave, desperate to be told a future he will not want to hear.

～ 19 ～

The Weakness of Power

Now when Pilate heard this, he was more afraid than ever. He entered his headquarters again and asked Jesus, "Where are you from?" But Jesus gave him no answer. Pilate therefore said to him, "Do you refuse to speak to me? Do you know that I have power to release you and power to crucify you?" Jesus answered him, "You would have no power over me unless it had been given you from above; therefore the one who handed me over to you is guilty of a greater sin." John 19:8–11

Suggested reading: John 18:28–19:16

In the relationships of professional life, weakness is very quickly revealed, but it may not be taken advantage of immediately. The knowledge may be stored away for future reference, and it may be used much later, but to devastating effect.

Pontius Pilate is an ideal example of how power and strength—particularly moral strength—do not necessarily always go together. His power was the result of his high office. A procurator in a province of the Roman empire held absolute power over the people he ruled, and was subject only to his superiors in Rome. Power came from the position, not from the inner quality of the man.

Pilate became procurator of Palestine in the year 26. The job was noted for being difficult. The country was volatile and unpredictable. Its Jewish leader, the high priest Caiaphas, was a brilliant politician and tactician, as Pilate was to discover early in his administration.

Already this Jewish province had managed to procure considerable concessions from the Roman authorities in applying the rules of Roman state religion. When Pilate arrived for the first time in Jerusalem—coming south from his official residence on the coast at Caesarea—he saw that, alone of all the main cities of the empire, Jerusalem was without a statue of the emperor.

Pilate immediately ordered his troops to carry and display the emperor's image on their standards. When they entered the Antonine tower, which overlooked the temple area, the troops were to place the images in such a way that they looked down into the temple area. This would be deeply offensive to the Jews. Pilate then returned to Caesarea, first having commanded that, if the Jews attacked the fortress, they were to be repulsed and, if necessary, killed.

But Pilate had grossly underestimated Caiaphas, the high priest. Pilate woke one morning in Caesarea to find about seven thousand Jews from Jerusalem occupying the area surrounding his residence. He ignored them, but they stayed. For a week Pilate endured the stand off. Still the great mass of people did not leave. Not only did they remain; they let him know that the steady drone of voices day and night was nothing less than prayers for his soul!

After a week had gone by, Pilate gave orders that the crowd should move to the city square—the agora, as Rome called this central area in a Roman city. As soon as the crowd had assembled, Pilate gave orders that the square was to be surrounded by troops fully armed and ready to kill. The procurator then announced his intention. Instead of retreating as expected, the Jews knelt, bearing their necks for slaughter. Pilate was defeated.

In the first year of their relationship, Caiaphas had taken stock of this Roman, had probed deeply for weakness, and had found it. The victory must have been sweet, both in itself and in what it promised for the future. Other incidents were to follow, when Pilate and Caiaphas would confront each other and the procurator would be defeated.

Pilate did not realize it, but he was now approaching events that would assure him a most unwelcome immortality. Once again a visit from Caiaphas was the prelude. There is the matter of a Galilean preacher, in Caiaphas's eyes a blasphemer and, if the procurator is prepared to look closely, also a potentially dangerous disturber of Roman order and peace. Step by step Pilate is manipulated, struggling like a fly in a web, only to enmesh himself further. He makes bombastic claims to authority that do nothing but reveal his lack of it. Even his quiet prisoner finds him singularly unimpressive.

The outcome was never really in doubt, as Caiaphas probably understood. By this time he knew his man for sure. One has a feeling, reading the text across the centuries, that Caiaphas almost plays with Pilate, allowing him room to struggle, but never really worries about the outcome. With a sudden reference to the emperor, the *coup de gras* is administered. "If you release this man, you are no friend of the emperor." Very few threats have been made with such economy of words and consummate timing, and few have been more effective. With a last whimper of defiance—"Shall I crucify your king?"—Pilate gives the fatal order to crucify, and the agony begins.

There is much said and written about the need to be aware of our strengths. We are told that we can give a great gift to another person when we point to his or her strengths. In doing so, we can sometimes release the other from such things as lack of self-confidence or lack of self-esteem and set them on the road to hope and achievement. But life is a matter of balance. It is equally true that we need to be aware of those things in which we are deficient.

Difficult though it may seem, we can benefit from getting to know our weaknesses, if only to avoid landing ourselves in situations where we cannot respond to our own or others' expectations. To accept our weaknesses—without underestimation or exaggeration—can be real wisdom. In this regard, a developed prayer life is invaluable. In the total intimacy between a Christian soul and God, we can fully acknowledge our weaknesses. To do so can be enriching and empowering.

～ 20 ～

The Greatest Gift

Love never ends. But as for prophecies, they will come to an end: as for tongues, they will cease; as for knowledge, it will come to an end. For we know only in part, and we prophesy only in part; but when the complete comes, the partial will come to an end.

1 Corinthians 13:8–10

Suggested reading: 1 Corinthians 13

In a moment of rare insight, Soren Kirkegaard observed that life is lived forward but understood backward. It is highly unlikely that this insight came to him before his fifties—I am guessing—but whenever it came, we are the richer for it. Its wisdom can be a gift to us.

We may have carried a regret for years, wishing that something had not happened, or that something had gone differently for us, until there comes a day—or even a moment—when we realize the blessings of what actually did happen. Such moments are beyond price. Through them, we come to understand the course of our life in a new way.

Like all of us, the man we know as Saul of Tarsus—later Paul the Apostle—is complex and many-layered. He has already experienced a radical redirecting of his life. Brilliant, articulate, energetic, and single minded, he has swung from being the implacable enemy of the new Christian faith to being its most formidable champion.

Paul's first great contribution to the new movement was to extend it beyond the boundaries of Palestine. For him, nothing less than the empire itself was a worthy object of mission. Over a period of about twenty years he showed extraordinary energy and courage, resulting in the formation of Christian communities in the cities of the Mediterranean world. To some of these he later wrote letters to address a specific problem in a community, or to explain some aspect of the faith, or to offer an outline of the meaning of the life, ministry, death, and resurrection of Jesus of Nazareth.

In one of these letters we are given a window into the soul of this great human being. Paul does not open many such windows, and so this one is all the more valuable. The insight occurs in probably the most difficult letter he ever had to write.

There are problems developing in Corinth that threaten the future of the Christian community. During the course of his letter, Paul points to the Christian virtues that should—but do not—characterize their life together. After a while he pauses, and then, as if coming to a decision, he writes, "I will show you a still more excellent way."

There follows what may be the finest passage Paul has ever written. It is certainly the most lyrical. He writes of the nature of love, and his words will probably be quoted as long as humanity longs and searches for that many faceted and powerful mystery we call love.

It is a commonplace to say that, whenever we risk writing our thoughts and feelings, we are always revealing more than we know. It is no different with Paul. "If I speak in the tongues of mortals and of angels ... if I have prophetic powers, and understand all mysteries and knowledge ... if I have all faith, so as to remove mountains, but do not have love, I am nothing."

A careful reading of this passage reveals something about the writer. Consciously or unconsciously—probably the latter—Paul is making a list of those gifts and strengths that are very much part of his own make up. He is wonderfully articulate. He has a magnificent mind. He has a powerful and intense faith and trust in God. He has shown an immense capacity to take physical punishment. Yet here we see him discounting the value of all these things when they are placed beside love as the bedrock of all motivation.

Are we overhearing a great man realizing and regretting a deficiency in his own make up? In writing to others, is he struggling to come to terms with a sense of loss in himself? Again, has he always been aware of this lack, or has it just surfaced? Paul is most certainly respected, probably even feared by some.

He must have known that his ability and strong leadership had gained him critics, if not enemies. In the dynamic of institutional life, this is unavoidable. He would also have known that he was held in great respect, even held in awe by some.

But is there any evidence to indicate that Paul was loved? The likelihood is remote. We have no evidence of Paul being dear to someone or they to him. There is of course the faithfulness of Luke and the eventual repair of the damaged relationship with Mark. There is the encouragement of, and admiration for, the young Timothy. But beyond these, there is no record of anything resembling a loving relationship.

We have to ask if we are hearing a regret, a longing for something in life that has remained unfulfilled, its presence unrecognized until now because of Paul's total commitment to his mission.

There is a saying that no one on their deathbed ever expressed a regret about not spending more time at the office. Are we hearing something like this from Paul? Is there a regret that he had not allowed an important part of his life to flower through the years? Did he come late to the understanding that all his achievement, great though it was, covered a deep wound in his heart—the inability to love and be loved?

All of us assess our lives at some point. All of us check the columns of plus and minus in the ledger of our lives—successes and failures, victories won and battles lost, hopes fulfilled and plans defeated. When we do so, it is important to realize that incompleteness is the norm for our humanity. To be human means to be incomplete. What enables us to make peace with our incompleteness is the realization that our being completed is the gift we receive only from a loving God, in whom all things find their completion.

~ 21 ~

An Uneasy Crown

Now Samuel had died, and all Israel had mourned for him and buried him in Ramah, his own city. Saul had expelled the mediums and the wizards from the land. The Philistines assembled, and came and encamped at Shunem. Saul gathered all Israel, and they encamped at Gilboa. When Saul saw the army of the Philistines, he was afraid and his heart trembled. When Saul inquired of the Lord, the Lord did not answer him.... Then Saul said to his servants, "Seek out for me a woman who is a medium."... His servants said to him, "There is a medium at Endor."
1 Samuel 28:3–7

Suggested reading: 1 Samuel 28:3–25

To be given great responsibility, and then to feel that one has failed in this trust, must be one of the heaviest burdens of life. If one has failed publicly, the personal agony is even greater.

Most of us do not have the opportunity to carry great responsibility or to occupy a very public stage in life. Most of us live reasonably modest lives where we try to be faithful to the important but limited duties of family and job. Perhaps this is the reason that we look with fascination when the great and famous encounter personal disaster, either financial or political.

In the tenth century BCE, Israel was at the stage of becoming conscious of itself as a single unified people. It would be some time before Israel would consider itself a nation in today's sense, but the urge to be other than a bundle of tribes had become strong. At this point, leadership was held by a powerful and charismatic figure whose role was a mingling of religious, social, judicial, and political qualities. His name was Samuel. He felt that the popular urge to crown a king as a unifying figure was unwise, but he gave in to public pressure. The one selected for this new role was a young man named Saul.

From the beginning Saul was a reluctant candidate. His position was not made easier by the fact that Israel faced a powerful enemy in its Philistine neighbours to the west and south. The threat of this rival power would overshadow Saul's reign, and he would never be entirely successful in dealing with it.

To compound Saul's task, his relationship with Samuel was a troubled one. In the eyes of the older man, the young king could do nothing well. Even a victory was not enough to earn the older man's respect. Why was it not a greater victory, a more complete one? Such was Samuel's attitude. It did not help that Samuel had never really approved of the new institution of monarchy and was showing signs of feeling that his own authority was being usurped

As time goes on, Saul, already unable to achieve a good relationship with his older rival, finds himself fighting on another relationship front. Into his court comes a young, brilliant, self-confident youth named David. Ironically it is Saul who invites him to court. Very soon the king realizes that he has invited into his life one who shows every sign of becoming a dangerous challenge to his authority. The danger becomes more obvious when David begins to grandstand in ways that bring him to public notice and even public admiration.

Try as he may, Saul cannot find a way to deal with this threat. Even the device of marrying David to his daughter Michal backfires. It not only adds to the alienation between himself and David, but damages Saul's relationship with his daughter. Finally the break is complete. David takes to the hills and becomes an explicit rival for power.

From this point on, Saul's defeat appears ever more certain. By now the king is showing signs of severe stress. His mood swings become more frequent, his headaches more agonizing. To augment his troubles, the Philistines once again open a campaign that needs to be addressed. The day is nearing when Saul must once again go to war.

The night before the battle, Saul panics. He decides to consult a soothsayer. Ironically, Saul has recently ordered all such people out of his kingdom! Now he finds himself at night facing a woman who is herself terrified when she realizes who has come to consult her.

Whether his overwrought state brings extraordinary images before him, or whether some traditional drug is applied, Saul encounters the spirit of the recently dead Samuel. To Saul's horror he hears his impending death prophesied for the morrow. He reels from the presence of the soothsayer, and the prophecy proves self-fulfilling. Within twenty-four hours Saul and his sons are dead on the battlefield.

Few of us achieve the prominence that Saul accepted and experienced. But because even the most prominent people share in our human nature, his tragic life addresses our lives. Was Saul a gifted and even charismatic ruler—at least in early days—who became the victim of an extraordinarily unfortunate cluster of circumstances, or was he a deeply flawed man who was doomed from the start? Can we even choose one of these possibilities over the other? His life is certainly a lesson in the way that early promise can be mistaken for mature staying power. His behaviour in the face of threats, personal or political, shows a deep insecurity underneath the trappings of power.

If nothing else, the life of Saul, king in Israel, suggests that we should probe very deeply into ourselves and others before accepting heavy responsibility. Perhaps the most necessary step is to take time to lay before God the responsibility that we are being offered. We need to measure its extent and its challenge and to look very carefully at our abilities and our ways of coping. Then, having done all this, we need to offer God the whole pattern—the nature of the challenge and our assessment of ourselves—and to ask for guidance. And, very important—we need to expect that guidance will be given.

Preserving Hope

Nothing is quite as moving as the faithfulness of a marriage partner to the other in the face of a debilitating condition, one that robs the marriage of many joys and activities usually taken for granted by others—the ability to travel or offer hospitality to friends. Such a situation reminds us that there is more than one kind of courage.

We tend to think of courage in terms of responding to sudden crisis, when we deal with the crisis in some way, if not solving it, at least lessening it. But beyond this kind of courage is what we might call "extended courage"—or even better, "resilience"—when we face not a sudden crisis but a long siege. Scripture introduces us to such people, men and women who have little choice but to carry a burden without any near hope of being able to get rid of it.

Michal, daughter of Saul the king, must carry the burden of being a woman when most of the conditions of a woman's life were circumscribed and dictated by men. Michal not only has a strong father, she also loves a man who will be even stronger. In this she confirms a pattern often seen in family life, where the charateristics of previous generations are perpetuated. Yet in spite of the many stresses she bears, Michal gives us the impression that she retains inner composure, and that she possesses strength to push back at the pressures placed on her.

As we have said, little can be more demanding than to endure a relentless physical condition that escapes remedy and saps the pleasure out of life. Scripture gives us the privilege of meeting a magnificent woman who is nameless. She has no choice but to bear a condition that robs her of much enjoyment in life. In the face of this condition, we see her show an unquenchable hope that eventually is rewarded in her encounter with Jesus.

Naaman too is afflicted with a condition that threatened to topple him from the height of power and influence to the horror of public banishment from society. It would seem that for some time he tries to hide what he dreads. Most of us can recall those times when we veer from the heights to the depths, as we think about some symptom or pain. At times we persuade ourselves that nothing is wrong; at other times we are engulfed by fear. Yet with support and direction from more than one unexpected source, Naaman is enabled to act and so to survive.

Bathsheba, wife of David and queen in Jerusalem, is easily associated with an incident that has grasped the imagination of generations. Her liaison with the young David is the only feature about her life that most people recall. More than anything else it identifies her and prevents her from being seen as the great human being she really is. In the face of loss, against the unrelenting pressure of being linked to a man of endless moods—not to mention the constant presence of other women in his life—Bathsheba retains her dignity and courage as the mother of a future king.

~ 22 ~

Resisting Domination

*Now Saul's daughter Michal loved David. Saul was
told, and the thing pleased him. Saul thought, "Let
me give her to him that she may be a snare for
him...."* 1 Samuel 18:20–21

*So David went and brought up the ark of God from
the house of Obed-Edom to the city of David with
rejoicing.... David danced before the ark with all his
might; David was girded with a linen ephod.... But
Michal the daughter of Saul came out to meet David,
and said, "How the king of Israel honoured himself
today, uncovering himself today before the eyes of his
servants' maids, as any vulgar fellow might shamelessly
uncover himself!" David said to Michal, "It was before
the Lord ... I will make myself yet more contemptible
than this, and I will be abased in my own eyes; but
by the maids of whom you have spoken, by them I
shall be held in honour."* 2 Samuel 6:12b–22

Suggested readings: 1 Samuel 18:20–29;
19:8–17; 2 Samuel 6:12–23

When we speak of oppression, we tend to think of it in political terms. But there is also a great deal of oppression experienced on the personal level of life. Sometimes we call it abuse, but this fails to fully explain what we can mean by oppression.

Abuse usually refers to particular acts or incidents. Oppression can involve few, if any, acts of overt abuse because it tends to be ongoing in a relationship. It can be so taken for granted that it becomes a norm, sometimes unrealized by the perpetrator but extremely costly to the victim. The contexts for oppression are many and varied. Spouses in a marriage, parents and children, employer and employees—all such relationships can lead to oppression.

Her name is Michal. She is the daughter of a king, and at some stage she will become the wife of an ambitious would-be king. She lives in a time and culture when women were regarded essentially as property, sometimes as very valuable property, through whom alliances could be made by marriage, regardless of the wishes or the happiness of the woman.

Michal's father is at that dangerous stage of political life when he still holds office but power is slipping away. Saul has been king for some years, and has been an able ruler. The tribes of Israel are by no means yet a nation. The person who will eventually give them a sense of nationhood is young but ambitious for Saul's throne. His name is David. He is one of those people who seem able to do whatever they wish in life. He has energy, courage, great self-confidence, driving ambition, and the ability to draw others around him. Gradually David emerges as a recognized, and eventually detested, rival for the throne.

All these complexities are further complicated by the fact that Michal falls in love with David—the nemesis of her father. Saul sets David what he thinks is an impossible task, as a condition for agreeing to the marriage. David performs the task with contemptuous ease. The wedding takes place.

It is quite possible that, in David, Michal saw an escape route from the oppressive situation of the king and his court. She soon finds that she has exchanged a strong father for a stronger husband, and that she must chose between them. When her father makes an attempt on David's life, she puts her own life on the line by warning David and allowing him to escape. It is the last she will see of him for some years. Instead she finds herself forced by her father to marry again, this time as he chooses.

As a guerrilla leader, David becomes strong enough to challenge the king's forces. Saul and his son Jonathan, a friend of David, die. David's first order is that Michal be found and brought to him. There is a pathetic scene when Michal approaches David with her husband trailing behind her, weeping and protesting until he is contemptuously dismissed.

Perhaps there was a short time of euphoric reunion, but Michal discovers that this new David is not to her liking. There is an extravagance, a consuming sense of self-importance, a liking for self-display. Michal is disgusted and expresses her disgust. She may have just realized that David is so consumed with himself that there is little room in his life for her or any other woman, other than as a transient sexual companion.

Michal leaves the stage of the story. She has survived both her father Saul and her husband, David, discovering that both of them—gifted and able though they appear—are also egotistical and domineering men. But though this woman's part in the long-ago drama is ended, we cannot help feeling that it ends on her terms and that she has preserved her integrity and the inner core of her being.

Sometimes there can be a temptation to accept the domination of another person. We can decide this because we love them, or because we feel we can change them, or because we are intimidated to the point of believing that we are helpless. Most often we will find that these strategies only encourage the other and ensure that the relationship continues on the same terms.

Best of all is to demonstrate that we are not just an extension of the other's will or wishes. We are not an object for their intimidation or manipulation. We too have a life, and we intend to live it on our terms. It is surprising how often—with much effort and after some resistance—a good relationship can develop.

～ 23 ～
A Quest for Healing

And a large crowd followed [Jesus] and pressed in on him. Now there was a woman who had been suffering from hemorrhages for twelve years. She had endured much under many physicians, and had spent all that she had; and she was no better but rather grew worse. She had heard about Jesus.

Mark 5:24b–27

Suggested reading: Mark 5:21–43

To spend years in any of the helping professions—as doctor, nurse, priest, social worker, counsellor, teacher, to name some—is to become aware of the extraordinary resilience of some human beings. It is humbling and inspiring to observe how certain men and women respond to unrelenting challenges. It is even more inspiring to see how, in the face of such challenges, some retain an unquenchable hopefulness.

Sometime during those months when Jesus was at the height of his popular acceptance and large crowds gathered around him, an incident took place that lets us glimpse the kind of person we have been thinking of—determined, resilient, hopeful. We meet her in the gospel. It may be significant that all three of the synoptic gospel writers recall this woman and her encounter with Jesus. That she remained in the memory of the Christian community is even more remarkable, since her story is introduced into the text almost as a parenthesis. It takes place as Jesus is responding to another plea for help, this time involving a seriously ill child.

For twelve years this woman has been struggling with an unusual menstrual flow that has robbed her of any pleasure in life. We need to realize how heavy a burden such a condition would have been in those days. Not only would she have known constant physical misery. She would have faced times of social restriction owing to the extent of the hemorrhaging. On many occasions she would have had to accept exclusion from the company of others.

We need to remind ourselves that twelve years in those days were a major part of one's life. And the very nature of her illness could have robbed her of the joys of marriage and children. We are not told whether there had been marriage and a family, but the circumstances in which we meet her in the gospel suggest a solitary life.

A Quest for Healing ⌣ 125

We get an indication of the kind of person she was when we are told, "she had endured much under many physicians, and had spent all that she had." Even though all of these efforts had produced no improvement, she is nevertheless determined to continue trying. We are in the presence of a courageous and determined woman.

Whether she is present in the crowd intentionally or has fortuitously found herself near this now well-known teacher, we don't know. What matters is the sudden realization that she must act, the sudden conviction that, if only she can touch him, even touch his clothes, her agony will end.

It is a mysterious moment that many people have known in different circumstances. Common to such moments is the sudden feeling of absolute certainty that one must act now and in a certain way if a great opportunity is not to be lost. The experience is mysterious because sometimes the action does bring about what is being sought or hoped for.

She pushes through the crowd. Anyone who has been in an excited Middle-Eastern crowd can imagine what a solitary woman must have done to make her way through it. Suddenly the visitor is within reach of her outstretched arm. There is no eye contact, something for which she may have been grateful because it might have weakened her resolve.

As soon as she touches the rough homespun robe, she knows with a surge of ecstatic certainty that something has happened in her body, utterly different from anything she can remember. She stands frozen in wonder, full of a joy that refuses to be repressed. As with any moment of ecstasy, time seems to stand still.

Suddenly she realizes that the rabbi is moving away from her. He is being swept along by the movement of the crowd.

But then she sees him stop. He begins to resist the crowd as it presses him toward the house where he has been summoned. She sees him calling out. At first she cannot hear him, but eventually she discerns the words, "Who touched my clothes?"

Those near him are puzzled by the question. Everyone has been pressing around him. How can it matter in the least who touched him? Jesus insists on knowing. The woman makes a decision. Going forward she kneels, not daring to engage face to face. As she does so, something lets her know that this man is prepared to listen. She tells her story, tells of the long years, of the sudden decision, the reaching out, the touching, the healing. And when she falls silent, she hears herself given peace and the assurance of healing.

Periods of clearly defined illness, bouts of great pain, occasions of great loss—all test us, sometimes almost beyond endurance. But even beyond these experiences lie the challenges of such things as a handicapped child whose needs will last beyond our own lifetime, a misshapen body we must inhabit for a lifetime, the gradual departure of a dearly loved partner into the hidden land of Altzeimer's disease where we cannot follow, except with the faithful love that must be offered without any discernible response.

Among those who face all of these immense challenges are some who seem to draw from a bottomless well of strength. While they may know moments of despair, they are never fully conquered by it. Among these extraordinary souls are those who will readily point to the source of that strength for them. In moments of prayer, moments of sacrament, moments of silence and stillness, they will know that they have touched, and have been touched by, their Lord.

～24～
Acknowledging One's Humanity

Naaman, commander of the army of the king of Aram, was a great man and in high favour with his master, because by him the Lord had given victory to Aram. The man, though a mighty warrior, suffered from leprosy.

Now the Arameans on one of their raids had taken a young girl captive from the land of Israel, and she served Naaman's wife. She said to her mistress, "If only my lord were with the prophet who is in Samaria! He would cure him of his leprosy."

2 Kings 5:1–3

Suggested reading: 2 Kings 5:1–14

Leadership is a most admirable human quality if exercised wisely and well. When present in an organization, community, or family, it can attract and inspire people, to the point where extraordinary things may be accomplished. Some may find themselves being moved to achieve far beyond any previous estimate of their potential. Others may discover gifts they had never realized they possessed. The highest quality of leadership can even inspire people to acts of great self-sacrifice.

There are many styles of leadership. Sometimes much can be achieved when different styles meet, blend, and cooperate in a task or project. But there is a certain kind of leadership that can become something else. Leadership that can act only by imposing its own will and vision soon crosses a line into domination. While at first much may seem to be gained, eventually a law of diminishing returns takes over and there is trouble. Sometimes the trouble first appears in the leader's own personal life and then becomes obvious to others.

The kingdom of Aram is a power to be reckoned with. In the ceaseless tribal warfare of the time, Aram's troops normally return home victorious. Its army forms a magnificent military machine. At the head of this machine is a gifted and battle-hardened veteran named Naaman who knows he has become indispensable to the royal house. Those around him see only immense courage and confidence. Only Naaman realizes that he may be paying a price for this carefully constructed image of an all-powerful leader.

What others do not see, because Naaman is not one to betray his inner feelings, is a man harbouring a deep fear that is becoming increasingly impossible to ignore. A skin lesion that has recently appeared on his body looks as if it may be leprosy. This could spell the end of his career. Naaman knows that even his military victories will count for nothing if the threat turns out to be true. Either he finds a cure or his career is ended.

Very few of us have not had a similar experience. Something is noticed and worry begins. It does not go away, and worry deepens. There are continual flashes of cold fear that even the busiest of lives cannot shut out. Eventually we are forced to act.

A young female slave in his wife's household makes a suggestion—not to Naaman, whom she would not have dared to address directly, but to his wife. The girl suggests that her master go to a healer in her own land of Israel. It is a measure of Naaman's desperation that he listens to this advice from one who is no more than an object in his house, over whom he has unquestioned power of life and death.

Asking for leave, Naaman sets out on his desperate quest. It is interesting how he travels. His entourage is huge and sumptuous, and this tells us much about him. Being an extension of Naaman, his entourage must above all else impress those to whom he is going.

On his arrival he receives a series of shocks. The local king, to whom he has a letter of introduction, is obviously terrified by his request, and regards it as a plot and a pretext for attack. When the royal court turns the formidable visitor over to a nearby holy man, Naaman gets another shock.

For years Naaman has become used to people responding to him as a figure of authority. But Elisha, the prophet to whom he has been directed, is not the least impressed. Shocks continue. When Naaman hears what he must do to seek healing—immerse himself in the rather pathetic flow of the nearby Jordan river—he is first appalled, then enraged.

All the frustration of the long journey, the poor reception, the disappointment of his desperate hopes, boils over. In a white heat of anger he turns on his heel and orders his entourage to leave.

Only the courage of a wise servant rescues the great man from his own pig-headedness. Gehazi knows his master well. If he counsels a change of mind, Naaman will fear this might be interpreted as a sign of weakness. Gehazi therefore flatters his master first, and only then advises discretion. After all, if the prophet had demanded that something difficult be done, of course the master could have done it. Why not therefore do the very simple thing that has been suggested? Gehazi is utter reasonableness.

Still blustering, Naaman follows the advice, turns around, swallows his dignity, and immerses himself in the Jordan. In the magnificent and lyrical language of scripture, "his flesh was restored like the flesh of a young boy."

An overbearing personality that can operate only by dominating others can eventually become self-defeating. Constantly preserving the image of command and authority can engender great stress. Eventually it takes a toll, as it did with Naaman. To modern minds his skin problems might even be recognized as a manifestation of extreme stress.

Leadership is a gift, and exercising it a vocation. Domination is a problem, both for ourselves and those around us. But through hearing and honouring what others think and say, such destructive leadership may eventually be healed.

～ 25 ～

The Years of Maturing

*So Bathsheba went to the king in his room. The king
was very old.... Bathsheba bowed and did obeisance
to the king, and the king said, "What do you wish?"
She said to him, "My Lord, you swore to your servant by the Lord your God, saying: Your son Solomon
shall succeed me as king, and he shall sit on my
throne. But now suddenly Adonijah has become
king, though you, my lord the king, do not know it....
But you, my lord the king—the eyes of all Israel are
on you to tell them who shall sit on the throne of my
lord the king after him. Otherwise it shall come to
pass, when my lord the king sleeps with his ancestors,
that my son Solomon and I will be counted offenders."*

1 Kings 1:15–21

Suggested reading: 1 Kings 1:1–31

One of the most common traps in our dealings with other people is to make snap decisions early in the relationship. Sometimes we make a decision about someone whom we have just encountered, a decision totally based on a first fleeting impression, and very often we can find out later that we have been quite wrong. The strange thing is that, no matter how often we are proved wrong, we continue to do this. The tendency can bedevil our personal, and sometimes our professional, relationships.

An ancient city was a place of great intimacy, especially for its ruling classes. The smallness of the area, the closeness of the houses, the narrowness of the streets—all combined to make for a cheek-by-jowl existence. The Jerusalem of David was no exception. We need to remind ourselves that the word "city" is rather misleading.

At this time Jerusalem was little more than a well-fortified encampment, its inhabitants sharing an intimacy from which there was no escape. Because of this, when the king walked on his rooftop in the late evening and saw an attractive woman a short distance away, it was not unusual. What was unusual was her beauty and the fact that she was bathing. The result is not only history but also the substance of some poor quality movies. The romance of David the king and Bathsheba, daughter of a senior royal advisor and wife of a senior army officer, has become legend.

The problem is that Bathsheba must forever play in this short and—for many—deliciously salacious scene. The truth of the matter, and the truth of Bathsheba—if we take the trouble to seek it—is very different. Her relationship with David does indeed begin with a passionate encounter, but we need to remember that in her society Bathsheba may well have been powerless to prevent the outcome, given the identity of her admirer.

In due time the encounter results in Bathsheba carrying David's child. Sadly the child dies, quite probably in Bathsheba's arms. She already has had to deal with the guilt that would have been unavoidable for a woman of her time and culture. Now she must deal with this terrible loss.

The couple weathers this loss of a beloved child. Both she and David rediscover their passion, and another child is born. Bathsheba remains faithful through much, including the reality that David involves himself with many women. She also bears the burden of the difficult years of David's struggle with his son Absalom, an experience that breaks David's heart.

Finally we meet Bathsheba in her later years. David, weak and ailing, has long let go the reins of empire. Even the knowledge that the rivalry among his sons endangers the queen's life fails to galvanize him into action. Bathsheba realizes that she is in a dreadfully exposed position. Finally she finds support in Nathan, the now aging prophet.

Bathsheba knows that, by the iron laws of her world, both she and her son Solomon will be slaughtered if a take-over succeeds. The old Nathan tells her that she must somehow wake David from his coma-like state and get him to name her son as king. For a long time David had promised her this, but he has never acted.

Coolly and courageously Bathsheba goes to her husband and succeeds in bringing him close enough to reality that he is able to understand the danger and to do what she wishes. As we listen to her words reported by the long-ago writer, we hear the sensitivity with which she approaches her ailing husband, even in the euphemistic language she uses to speak of the dreadful danger threatening her and Solomon her son. "Solomon and I shall be counted offenders," she says quietly, meaning that she and Solomon will be slaughtered. It is almost the last we see of this able and resilient woman. For some years she will live on in the court of her son Solomon, respected as queen dowager.

How different a character we now see in Bathsheba—utterly different from the image based on a single early episode of her life. To judge her by those first impressions would be to miss the qualities still hidden in the future. Yet many people who read scripture do this to Bathsheba. And in the course of daily life, many of us do it to each other.

If we perceive a pattern in ourselves of dismissing others too easily on first impression, we need to curb this tendency. Sometimes much can depend on our not being dismissive of others—the child we are teaching, the doctor we are choosing for ourselves or our family, the person we are interviewing for a job being offered.

In every case we can so easily make hasty decisions that may deprive the other of an all-important opportunity, and may deprive ourselves of their gifts in our lives. Perhaps a moment's recalling that God has so far not dismissed us, in spite of all our shortcomings, might temper our dismissing of others on first impression.

In Lasting Friendship

"Friendship is valuable precisely because it is so precarious: one well-timed joke can establish it, one cutting remark can end it.... With old friends you have come up against the incorrigible in one another."

So wrote Michael Ignatieff in an essay on friendship entitled "Lodged in the Heart and Memory." Perhaps the most significant word in this statement is "incorrigible." The test of friendship is to have encountered the incorrigible in the other and, in spite of it, to stay with the relationship. By staying we give one of life's most precious gifts—the knowledge that there is someone—apart from spouse or partner—with whom a person can be utterly honest and natural.

Scripture is rich in descriptions of many friendships. In the first years of the very early Christian communities that we glimpse in the letters of Paul, groups are forming where deep friendships are flowering—among the members and with Paul himself—even as he comes and goes among these communities. Church life today, whether in small or large congregations, is the seedbed of countless friendships, some lasting a lifetime in spite of separations.

The bonds between Jesus and his disciples exhibit many elements of friendship, particularly in the inner circle of Peter,

James, and John, and even beyond this, with Peter himself. To recognize this is to realize even more fully the humanity our Lord shares with us.

The bond between Elijah and Elisha is that between younger student and older mentor. In recent years the bond has been forged, but the older man has come to discover that there is a great deal of dependency in the relationship. Elijah realizes that Elisha is finding it very difficult to accept mature responsibility. There are repeated efforts to sever the bond, not because of rejection, but because of Elijah's concern for his younger colleague. The one thing that holds firm throughout the difficult process of severance is the relationship between the two.

David the king and Joab the general go back a long way. They knew each other when they roamed the south Judean hills as young guerrilla fighters. Theirs is a long and proven friendship. In their later years there comes a moment when the depth of this friendship allows Joab to save David from being consumed by personal grief. Joab administers a rebuke that must have been shocking to David both in its harshness and its unexpectedness. The language is stark, even brutal, and the tone of voice was probably just as severe. Joab must have known that he was taking a great risk, but their friendship proves strong enough to achieve the desired effect. David rallies and manages to hold on to public respect.

When a widow and her widowed daughter-in-law return to the family lands of the former, they have no idea what lies ahead. They are utterly at the mercy of circumstances. As it happens, the lives of Naomi and Ruth are transformed. First they find hospitality and then great happiness. Ruth's joy is in discovering that she is loved; Naomi's joy is for Ruth's good fortune. But the one constant through all through this story is the relationship of the two women. Each is totally committed to the other in an unbreakable bond of loving friendship.

～ 26 ～

A Longing for Companionship

The next day John [the Baptist] again was standing with two of his disciples, and as he watched Jesus walk by, he exclaimed, "Look, here is the Lamb of God!" The two disciples heard him say this, and they followed Jesus....

One of the two who heard John speak and followed him was Andrew, Simon Peter's brother. He first found his brother Simon and said unto him, "We have found the Messiah" (which is translated Anointed). He brought Simon to Jesus, who looked at him, and said, "You are Simon son of John. You are to be called Cephas" (which is translated Peter).

John 1:35–42

Suggested reading: John 1:35–42 and
Matthew 4:18–22

"Those friends thou hast, and their adoption tried, grapple them to thy soul with hoops of steel." Such is Hamlet's advice to Horatio, and good advice it is. Part of the process of our maturing is the realization that friendship does not just happen. Perhaps the initial possibility happens. Two people meet and some spark is ignited, there comes a sense of being on a wavelength, a natural feeling of companionship, just enough to suggest there is something worth pursuing. But if there is to be a lasting friendship, it must be a work in progress.

We tend to neglect the role of friendship in Jesus' life, especially the few short years of his public life. We know there were disciples, but we tend not to think of these imagined faces and voices as friends. We see them following, listening, asking questions, discussing, even arguing among themselves. But such is not quite the stuff of friendship. Friendship is where each has need of the other, draws upon the other, each giving and receiving.

If we look closely, there is evidence of friendship, evidence that adds to the portrait of Jesus' full humanity, assuring us that nothing in our human experience has not been shared by our Lord.

We are quick to assume that Jesus' decision to involve others, to build a band of disciples, was to bring into being an embryonic church or fellowship. So it may have been. But it may also have been that, to carry out his purpose and bring his vision to reality, he needed friends. These he discovers along the small jetty at the head of the lake. First the two brothers Simon and Andrew; very soon after, another two, James and John.

Soon there are others whose names we know well, but

there remains something special about his relationship with these early companions. Andrew is often the go-between for those who want to approach to Jesus, and this suggests that an easy natural bond had formed very early in the relationship. It is Andrew who finds the boy who will supply the meagre food for the vast crowd, Andrew who introduces Jesus to a group of Greeks seeking to meet the by now well-known rabbi, and, in John's gospel, it is Andrew who introduces his brother Peter to his own new-found friend.

But it is the threesome of Peter, James, and John, to whom Jesus turns most naturally for friendship. Called to respond to the sickness of the daughter of a local official, Jesus takes the three into the house. They accompany him on the mysterious episode we call his transfiguration, and it is these three whom he allows to share his agony in Gethsemane.

Even within this small circle there is a greater depth of friendship—that with Peter. There is something hinting of an attraction of opposites in this relationship. The serenity and quiet thoughtfulness of the one, the impetuous emotional reactions of the other. If there is indeed a quality of opposites in the friendship, it shows itself on more than one occasion in misunderstandings and even sharp rebukes.

Jesus' attempt in Caesarea Philippi to communicate the danger and the cost of what he was about is countered by Peter's refusal to consider such things. Jesus' curt and dismissive response to his friend is a measure of his frustration with such inability to understand. There is the same suggestion of impatience with Peter's inability to see the all-important lessons of servanthood in Jesus' asking for his foot to be extended for washing.

In Gethsemane, surrounded by the temple police, Jesus

sharply rebukes Peter for lashing out at one of the guards. We have only to recall the look that passes between them across the courtyard fire in the high priest's house, a moment sufficient to send Peter into the night weeping. A last moment on the lakeshore, when the risen Christ sits with his old friend and gives him back his courage and his leadership—even then there is a hint of impatience with Peter's nervousness about the younger and more intuitive John, as he approaches across the beach.

And yet this friendship lasts. In spite of Peter's difficulty in understanding this friend who had entered and transformed his simple work-a-day life, he remains faithful into old age and even in the ultimate test of martyrdom.

Lasting friendship must become resilient in the face of many things. A disagreement when words are sharply exchanged, a period of seeming neglect, sometimes for valid reasons realized only later. If at all possible, work must constantly be done. Contact must be kept up—something often difficult in a world of constant travel, relocations in professional life, stressful times when there is little opportunity for other than survival.

Ironically these are the very reasons for making sure that friendship is nurtured and, at the same time, the reasons why it can so easily be neglected. Enrichment of a relationship can come from the simplest of things—a phone call, an e-mail, a card from some place we are travelling, a message sent through a mutual acquaintance met at a conference.

We make many investments in life, in all of them hoping for reward and even riches. There comes a time when we realize that investment in our friendships can bring riches beyond counting, and can be among God's most precious gifts to us.

~ 27 ~

A Discovery of Maturity

Now when the Lord was about to take Elijah up to heaven by a whirlwind, Elijah and Elisha were on their way from Gilgal. Elijah said to Elisha, "Stay here, for the Lord has sent me as far as Bethel." But Elisha said, "As the Lord lives, and as you yourself live, I will not leave you." 2 Kings 2:1–2

Suggested reading: 2 Kings 2:1–16

In human life maturing is always more a process than a state of being. We don't wake up one day with the knowledge that we have achieved maturity, at least not full maturity. As long as we live, we are striving to become more mature—occasionally failing, sometimes succeeding.

Maturity does not come as a free gift. It is forged in the living of a life. Sometimes that forging can be joyful, and sometimes it can be very painful. It may be that we have to endure the experience of watching those whom we love being forced to mature as they respond to some challenge life is throwing at them.

There may be times when we realize that we have sheltered someone too much and thus made it more difficult for them to mature. This is probably part of the issue in this magnificent scripture—the telling of a young man's struggle for maturity, and the efforts of an older man to make this possible.

For more than a generation a deep disagreement has disturbed the life of the people of Israel. At issue is a decision about the name and the nature of God. This means, of course, that they are arguing about the nature of reality itself. What kind of a world are we in? How does it work? What does it mean to live in that world? How do we name God?

They face a choice between two concepts of God. Some say that God is a God of nature and that his name is Baal. Others say that God is more than a God of nature. He is also a God of history, and his name is Yahweh. Much more depends on this choice than just naming. If the name of God is Baal, then reality is to be viewed as cyclic, reflecting much of nature—the cycle of the Moon, the return of the Sun, the round of the seasons. If God is to be named Yahweh, then life is to be seen as essentially progressive—a line from past to present to future.

Elijah is the great champion of the Yahweh side. He is getting old, and he knows this. For the last few years he has been training a younger man with a name very like his own—Elisha. The older man realizes that the time is very near when the younger must accept full responsibility for the struggle. Unfortunately the younger man is showing every sign of not being ready.

Elijah begins his efforts to transfer authority by trying to detach himself for short periods of time. Every time he attempts this, the younger man pleads to stay with him, and the older man begins to despair of effecting the transfer.

Time goes by. Elijah becomes increasingly aware of the urgency of the situation. He knows that some opportunity must be found to deal with the younger man's fears. There comes a day when the two of them are walking somewhere in the Jordan valley. Without warning, the older man turns, looks full in the eyes of the younger, and with almost brutal directness announces the nearness of his own death. At the same time he asks what the younger wishes from him before he dies. Elisha is panic-stricken. Hardly knowing what he is saying, he pleads that he may be given twice the gifts, confidence, authority, and ability of his mentor.

There is a moment of silence. Elijah knows this moment can be one of either breakthrough or failure. Forcing himself to be gentle and reasonable, he tells Elisha that everything will depend on how he faces his mentor's approaching death. If Elisha runs, all will be lost. If he stands his ground, then he will find within himself what neither Elijah nor anyone else can give him—the gifts, abilities, and the inner integrity that will make it possible for him to be a worthy successor in the life of his people.

As with many such moments the issue is not resolved immediately. The two continue to work together, but soon afterward Elijah dies. Elisha almost howls his agony and loss. Distractedly he hugs to himself the robe of his dead mentor. Then something beautiful takes place. He has always equated Elijah's authority with the older man's ability to know the crossing places on the river. Elisha walks toward the water, hesitates in indecision and fear, then walks forward. There is a simple but powerful phrase in the biblical story. It says simply, "Elisha went over."

In the sense that we spend our lives achieving maturity, then it is true for all of us that we spend our lives "going over." We go over from childhood to youth, from innocence to sophistication, from youth to adulthood, on through middle years, to senior years and old age. We spend our lives going over from such things as despair to hope, from anger to forgiveness, from alienation to reconciliation. As we do this in our own experience we help others to do it in their experience.

As parents we strive to help our children in their times of "going over." As teachers and mentors we work to make times of "going over" possible for others. As friends we try to help others. And sometimes we try to open ourselves to accept help in our own, sometimes painful, times of going over. Life is a journey in which God calls us continually toward an ever-deepening maturity.

~ 28 ~

A Moment of Honesty

*[Joab said to David:] "So go out at once and speak
kindly to your servants; for I swear by the Lord, if
you do not go, not a man will stay with you this
night; and this will be worse for you than any disaster that has come upon you from your youth until
now." Then the king got up and took his seat in the
gate.* 2 Samuel 19:7–8

Suggested reading: 2 Samuel 18:1—19:8

The term *ainmcara* has become familiar in recent years. It is really the marriage of two Gaelic words, *ainm* meaning "soul or spirit"—interestingly it can also mean "name"—and *cara* meaning "friend." Usually the term is expressed in English as soul-friend. The term comes from the six and seventh centuries in Ireland. It was important for the Christian spirituality of the time that one should have a soul-friend, an intimate relationship in which things of the spirit could be shared.

There is a moment in scripture when we see one of the necessary—though not always appreciated—roles of such a friend magnificently acted out, even at some risk to the friendship itself. It takes place late in the life of David, king in Israel.

For some years David has refused to acknowledge a grim reality that is becoming more and more a threat to his throne. His son Absalom has grown increasingly disaffected from his father. He has also become ambitious, envying his father the kingdom and waxing increasingly determined to take it. Eventually Absalom leads a rebellion.

That his son should do this was deeply distressing to the sensitive, sometimes even sentimental, David. For quite some time the king remains in denial about the threat to his throne. When eventually his advisors, chief among them his friend Joab, insist that something must be done, David agrees but with reservation. Scripture seems to suggest that he is strangely detached, as if unable to deal with the situation.

"Whatever seems best to you, I will do," David says to Joab. He gives permission for a campaign to begin, but hedges Joab's mission with the almost plaintive plea, "Deal gently for my sake with the young man Absalom." It is significant that, even at this point, David cannot bring himself to refer to this rival for power as his son. Absalom has become for his father "the young man."

The campaign is successful in that Absalom's forces are overcome. While fleeing, Absalom is caught in the branches of a tree. Joab's junior officers are unwilling to dispatch Absalom because no one knows how David will react. Only when Joab himself takes responsibility for the fatal spear thrust do others join the slaughter.

Meanwhile David anxiously awaits news of the battle, including news of his beloved but traitorous son. When that news eventually arrives, the king is devastated. He moves into his private quarters and bursts into wild and passionate lament. Even from the few words given to us by the historian it is obvious that David is overcome with intense parental sorrow, guilt, and despair. "O my son Absalom, my son, my son Absalom! Would I had died instead of you, O Absalom, my son, my son!"

Within an hour or two the bulk of the successful loyalist army returns. They have made it possible for David to remain on his throne. Without them he would by now be a fugitive fleeing for his life. In spite of this, there is no sign of David. He is still in his private quarters unable to function, utterly absorbed in his private grief.

Swiftly word spreads that the king is capable of nothing more than mourning. The morale of the returning troops is affected. There is no victory parade, no public speeches of congratulation and gratitude. In a vivid image we are told, "The troops stole into the city that day as soldiers steal in who are ashamed when they flee in battle." Centuries later any veteran of the tragic Vietnam war would understand this statement to his pain and cost.

It is Joab who acts, swiftly and decisively. Even at the risk of losing his rank and perhaps his life, he demands an audience with David. As Joab enters the king's quarters, he can hear David still weeping and calling Absalom's name. Joab storms into the room and scathingly berates David. He points out that a company of brave men have risked their lives for David's throne and he has not even had the grace to thank them.

"You have made it clear," Joab declares, "that commanders and officers are nothing to you, for I perceive that if Absalom were alive and all of us were dead today, then you would be pleased." Shocked out of his self-absorption, David emerges and responds publicly as he should have done in the first place.

As with many things, recent Western cultural usage has softened—perhaps even cheapened—the concept of soul-friend. It is spoken of nowadays mainly in terms of one giving the other support, comfort, understanding, and affirmation. Of course, these things are a necessary and admirable part of friendship, but a very important and valuable part of the original concept has been lost. While the soul-friend relationship certainly did comprise these aspects, it also included the necessity to question the friend's thinking or behaviour, even to correct and—when necessary—to criticize and to challenge.

In this way the tradition of *ainmcara* includes—and perhaps reflects—our relationship with God, a relationship where nothing need be hidden, if only because nothing can be hidden.

∼ 29 ∼

A Loving Faithfulness

Do not press me to leave you or to turn back from
*   following you!*
Where you go, I will go;
Where you lodge, I will lodge; your people shall be
*   my people, and your God my God.*
Where you die, I will die—there will I be buried.
May the Lord do thus and so to me, and more as
*   well,*
if even death parts me from you! Ruth 1:16–17

Suggested reading: Book of Ruth

In one of his novels Ernest Hemingway has a character say, "Life breaks us all, and some become strong at the jagged edges." The mystery is why some of us become strong under adversity, while others are broken, sometimes irreparably. A further mystery is that those we think will be strong are often least capable of showing strength, while those we have tended to see as weak show themselves to be spiritual giants.

The search for what can make the difference between being empowered by life's challenges or being seriously damaged leads us to a woman in Holy Scripture. We meet her soon after she has suffered the ultimate loss not only of her husband but of her children.

Her name is Naomi, and we meet her first in her years of happiness and fulfillment. She is married, and she and her husband Elimelech have two boys named Mahlon and Chilion. When the shadow of famine looms over the Bethlehem countryside, they have the youthful energy to up stakes and head for what look like greener pastures. With high hopes the family emigrates across the Jordan river into the area then called Moab.

All goes reasonably well for a decade or so. Then Elimelech dies quite suddenly. It would appear that the boys are old enough to carry the family's welfare. They eventually marry local young women, Orpah and Ruth. Once again the future looks bright, only to be devastated by the deaths of both young husbands.

In that long-ago society a widow needed the protection and support of her extended family. Here were three women, all widowed, one a foreigner. The society around them would have felt no obligation either to their welfare or their safety. In desperation Naomi decides to seek assistance and some measure of security by returning to her own extended family around Bethlehem. Her two daughters-in-law insist on coming with her, an offer Naomi accepts at first but later rejects. She eventually persuades Orpah to stay with her own people, but she fails to get Ruth to leave her.

We share the anxious, even desperate, conversation between the aging Naomi and her daughters-in-law. The older woman's great fear is that these two young women now risk the same fate as herself if they return to the Bethlehem area with her. They will in turn find themselves widowed in a society that will regard them as foreigners. There may be scant respect for them, perhaps even exploitation.

Naomi pleads with the two to go back into Moab. There too they are vulnerable as widows, but at least they are not foreigners. The conversation ends with Orpah's decision to return to Moab and Ruth's insistence on staying with her mother-in-law. Her insistence is expressed in one of the loveliest passages in scripture, quoted above. Bidding farewell to the departing Orpah, Naomi and Ruth turn toward the river and begin their journey to Bethlehem.

Is it possible to see in the eloquent and moving response of Ruth, the first source of returning hope and life in Naomi? At the moment of utter despondency, when she thinks she is about to bid farewell to the very last links with remembered years of fleeting family joy, Naomi finds herself being assured of love and faithfulness beyond all her expectation. Scripture gives us no reply of Naomi to Ruth's magnificent statement of loyalty, probably because no words were necessary. All that could or should be said had been said. The consequences of those words and that loyalty would be acted out in the months to come.

During those weeks and months we see this broken aging woman come alive. She becomes a person of focused energy and determined purpose. She has decided to live for her daughter-in-law's happiness. This she achieves through wise advice and gentle encouragement. Naomi pours herself into Ruth's quest for love and fulfillment, and in the success of that quest both women share, as they had shared in sorrow and loss.

Is it possible that we see in this wonderful book of the Bible at least some of the ways in which we can help each other to recover from tragedy, pain, and loss? How life changing it can be for someone to realize that they are not entirely alone, that they have not lost all, that there is at least one person who passionately believes in them and is prepared to be loyal to them!

There is the other side of this realization. Sometimes, after we ourselves have suffered, we may come to realize that there is someone who needs us as we need them. But to help them we need first to emerge from the suffering that threatens to immobilize us, and become engaged in the challenges that they must face and the choices they must, with our help, make. To discover this can be empowering and grace giving.

Lectionary References

The following table shows the **Day** of the liturgical year, the **RCL** (Revised Common Lectionary) scripture citation, the **Page Number** in *Living Scripture,* and the **Passage** of scripture linked with the reflection.

Year A

Day	RCL	Page	Passage
Lent 5	Ezek 37.1–14	20	Ezek 37.13–14
Holy Saturday	1 Pet 4.1–8	44	1 Pet 4.7–11
Easter Vigil	Ezek 37.1–14	20	Ezek 37.13–14
Proper 2	Jn 1.29–42	140	Jn 1.35–42
Proper 3	Mt 4.12–23	140	Mt 4.18–22
Proper 25	Ex 16.2–15	28	Ex 16.2–10
Proper 33	Judg 4.1–7	32	Judg 4.1–4

Year B

Day	RCL	Page	Passage
Easter Vigil	Ezek 37.1–14	20	Ezek 37.13–14
Easter 6	Acts 10.44–48	12	Acts 10.44–48
Holy Saturday	1 Pet 4.1–8	44	1 Pet 4.7–11
Trinity Sunday	Is 6.1–8	56	Is 6.1–5
Pentecost	Ezek 37.1–14	20	Ezek 37.13–14
Proper 2	1 Sam 3.1–10 (11–20)	80	1 Sam 3.1–5
Proper 4	1 Sam 3.1–20	80	1 Sam 3.1–5
Proper 6	2 Kings 5.1–14	128	2 Kings 5.1–3
Proper 13	Mk 5.21–43	124	Mk 5.24b–27

Year B continued

Year C

Path Books
A LIGHT TO MY PATH

We hope that you have enjoyed reading this Path Book. For more information about Path Books, please visit our website at **www.pathbooks.com.** If you have comments or suggestions about Path Books, please write us at publisher@pathbooks.com.

Other Path Books

God with Us: The Companionship of Jesus in the Challenges of Life *by Herbert O'Driscoll.* In thirty-three perceptive meditations, Herbert O'Driscoll considers the challenges of being human, searches key events in the life of Jesus, and discovers new vitality and guidance for our living. He shows us how the healing wisdom and power of Jesus's life can transform our own lives today.
1-55126-359-9 $18.95

Sacred Simplicities: Seeing the Miracles in Our Lives *by Lori Knutson.* In these engaging, two-page stories, Knutson shares her experience of the divine in the everyday, helping us to see glimpses of God where we least expect them. Enrichment for time at home or while travelling, meditations with nature, or sermon illustrations.
1-55126-419-6 $18.95

Christ Wisdom: Spiritual Practice in the Beatitudes and the Lord's Prayer *by Christopher Page.* The Beatitudes and the Lord's Prayer offer us a profound challenge to live in intimate communion with God. This pastorally-oriented book aims to help us discover new insights in Jesus's teaching. Each chapter includes reflective questions and spiritual exercises to help integrate the teachings into everyday life. *1-55126-420-X $16.95*

The Word Today: Reflections on the Readings of the Revised Common Lectionary *by Herbert O'Driscoll.* "These volumes will not only be of immense help to clergy in sermon preparation, but also for interested laity hoping to deepen their understanding of scripture and theology"— BARRY HENAULT.

Year A, Vol 1: 1-55126-331-9 $14.95
Year A, Vol 2: 1-55126-332-7 $14.95
Year A, Vol 3: 1-55126-333-5 $18.95
Year B, Vol 1: 1-55126-334-3 $14.95
Year B, Vol 2: 1-55126-335-1 $14.95
Year B, Vol 3: 1-55126-336-X $18.95
Year C, Vol 1: 1-55126-337-8 $14.95
Year C, Vol 2: 1-55126-338-6 $14.95
Year C, Vol 3: 1-55126-339-4 $18.95

*Available from your local bookstore or
Anglican Book Centre, phone 1-800-268-1168
or write 80 Hayden Street, Toronto, ON M4Y 3G2.*